THE TAO OF
CHIP
KELLY

LESSONS FROM AMERICA'S
MOST INNOVATIVE COACH

MARK SALTVEIT

DIVERSIONBOOKS

For Anna and Rose, my best readers,
and for Olga, my sharpest editor.

Diversion Books
A Division of Diversion Publishing Corp.
443 Park Avenue South, Suite 1004
New York, New York 10016
www.DiversionBooks.com

For more information, email info@diversionbooks.com

First Diversion Books edition December 2013.

Print ISBN: 978-1-62681-226-0
eBook ISBN: 978-1-62681-225-3

CONTENTS

Introduction

Chip Kelly's plays and schemes will change now that he has moved from the University of Oregon to the Philadelphia Eagles. They'll probably change from game to game, and quarter to quarter.

But underneath the winning strategies that baffle his opponents, there is a remarkably consistent and surprisingly profound philosophy—a philosophy that will work for any leader or manager. Kelly's biggest innovations don't involve football tactics at all. They are ways to clarify and communicate a vision for your team, an understanding of the prime importance of executing your plans, and a system for building a powerful humility into the structure of your organization.

By a lucky coincidence, these innovations also produce exciting football teams that destroy opponents.

Certainly Kelly's record of success is astonishing by any measure. As offensive coordinator at the University of New Hampshire, his teams consistently set offensive records and attracted attention from coaching geeks around the country.

Before Kelly was hired as head coach, Oregon had last won a Rose Bowl in 1917, and to this day the Ducks can't compete with the big football powers in recruiting top talent. Yet Kelly's teams went 46-7 over four years, with a BCS Bowl game every year and top-5 national rankings his last three years.

Only one other team—three-time national champion Alabama, at 49-5—has been as consistent during that time, and the SEC powerhouse's tremendous recruiting advantage makes Nick Saban's achievement less impressive.

Others have written about Chip Kelly's strategy and results

in great detail. This book aims to sketch the outlines of Chip Kelly's philosophy, using his own words from interviews and press conferences wherever possible. It also relies on the only three things he has published—his lectures at Nike's Coach of the Year workshop in 2009, 2011, and 2012.[1] These are essential reading for any students of Chipism.

Coach Kelly has not structured his philosophy into any organized framework. He teaches with parables and mottoes, so I have built this book around those.

I'm not sure he has systematically laid out his philosophy even in his own mind, and that is part of his strength. He is relentlessly focused on what works, as tested again and again by real world results. As soon as you paint a big picture by connecting all these little truths, you run the risk of drifting away from those results into words and ideas that are perfectly logical and orderly—but may not reflect the messy realities of life. That's a mistake that Kelly never makes.

However, most of us don't have twenty years of sixteen-hour days to devote to developing a fiercely reality-based and innovative system. So I'm taking the risk of oversimplifying Kelly's insights in order to highlight the innovations of one of America's most successful and underappreciated managers.

The unique achievement of Chip Kelly is that he is able to combine innovative strategy with a compelling underlying philosophy and a ruthless commitment to testing both against real world results. He has the humility to adjust his philosophy and strategy without attachment to his own ideas, no matter how successful they've been in the past.

All coaches—Chip included—have good seasons and disappointing ones, upsets and miracles. The best poker players lose a lot, too. But they win a little more on good hands and lose a little less with bad ones. Sometimes they scheme their way to victory when they have no business hoping to win. They can't control what happens, but they have learned to nudge the odds in their favor.

That is what Kelly does on the football field. He is not a genius, guru, or wizard, as much as the media likes to push that angle (and then turn around and shoot it down).

More than anything, he is an innovative manager who has learned to thrive at the highest levels of football's controlled chaos, and his insights are useful to anyone interested in building an elite organization.

He also has fun with his teams, and as a result, they are fun to watch. That may ultimately be the most important lesson of his success.

Portland, Oregon
December 2013

THE PROGRAM

Chapter 1
Win the Day®

Chip Kelly's most famous motto is found everywhere in Eugene, Oregon—on caps and T-shirts, billboards and walls, and stadiums. The University of Oregon even trademarked it.

Why not? It's working for them.

But the concept is more than just a catchy slogan, a modern update of Nike's "Just Do It.®" This phrase is at the core of Chip's personal philosophy, a down-to-earth New England version of what a California Buddhist might call mindfulness, or being present.

> "We live in the moment. Our football team lives in the moment…The only thing we can control is today. I'm always worried about today."[2]

A Chinese sage said, "The journey of a thousand miles begins with a single step."[3] That's in there, too. The flip side of that message is that you have to complete each one of those steps first before you get to the end of the one thousand miles. The way you go 12-0 in the regular season, as Oregon did in 2010, is to win each game, one at a time. Not by looking ahead.

> "I think people too often look way down the road—you know, 'I want to do this, I want to do that, I want to be conference champion, national champion.' If you don't take care of Tuesday, that's not going to happen."[4]

Win The Day!® also includes Kelly's focus on practicing hard and well. Everyone tries to win game days, but most days are for practice. The key to success is winning those Tuesdays and Wednesdays and Thursdays.

There's a lot more packed into those three simple words—all the hard work, the attentiveness, the relentless focus on execution that drives Kelly's success. For a smart guy with a lot of original concepts, Kelly has a laser-like focus on tangible results. Ideas don't matter until you carry them out.

Win The Day!® began in New Hampshire, when Kelly was an assistant coach there, as a way to liven up long spring practices. It was actually a contest, where one player at each position "won" each day. Chip brought it with him to Oregon and gave it a more general meaning. He told the *Oregonian* newspaper that fans tell him

> "that's their philosophy and that they try to apply it to their life. Because it's not about football. It's about everything you do. That encourages me, that they can look to our team and find something that's inspirational to them."[5]

Winning the day isn't quantitative. There's no need to keep charts of days lost and won. At a press conference on New Year's Eve, just before the 2012 Rose Bowl game, Kelly was asked how many days he won in 2011. "I don't know," he said. "I'm not that anal."[6] This is an attitude about right now.

A big part of winning the day is not worrying about the future. And Kelly lives by this mantra himself. Almost as soon as he took over in Philadelphia, he was peppered with daily questions about who the starting quarterback would be—Michael Vick? Nick Foles? Matt Barkley or Dennis Dixon? Chip was having none of it.

> "One of the things that allows me to think outside the box is I never deal with hypotheticals. You'll kill yourself. I could have nine million different scenarios today, on March 20, what if Michael does this, what if Nick does this, and what if Dennis gets in the mix, and then what if Trent Edwards, and what if we draft a quarterback? I don't deal

with that, I just deal with what the reality is."[7]

It also means not worrying about the past. The Eagles are paying Kelly $6.5 million a year to coach.[8] Just six years ago, he was making $62,000 a year—less than 1/100th as much—as an assistant coach at the University of New Hampshire. And by all accounts, he was perfectly happy.[9]

In 2006, a year before Chip went to Oregon, New York Giants coach Tom Coughlin offered him an assistant coaching job. Though he has "the utmost respect" for Coughlin, Kelly turned it down because it was a quality control job, not position coaching, and he didn't want to stop working directly with players. After he was hired in Philly, a reporter asked if he regretted that decision to pass on the job with the Giants.

> "No. I've always said before, the big time's where you're at, so if you're happy, and I was extremely happy where I was, I'm not a big second-guess guy."[10]

Charles Fischer is the chief analyst at FishDuck.com, a leading Oregon Ducks strategy website. (Full disclosure: I write for the site.) He told me that if Oregon's Mike Bellotti hadn't actively recruited Kelly, he thinks Chip would still be an assistant coach at New Hampshire, underpaid, working fourteen-hour days, setting offensive records, and enjoying the hell out of himself.[11]

Because *that* is how you Win The Day! ®

Chapter 2
The Vision: Fast. Play Hard. Finish.

Chip Kelly is not the sort of coach who just collects successful plays and schemes to use. Each of his teams has a comprehensive football program that starts with a cohesive vision, defined by Kelly and clearly communicated to the players.

Kelly's vision includes an effort to grab every advantage possible before the game even starts. This means a sophisticated understanding of the relation of practice to on-field performance as well as science-based guidelines for players' ideal nutrition, sleep and conditioning.

The basic concepts are simple, but the vision is deep, and implementation is complex. One of Chip's greatest gifts is an ability to boil down these complicated ideas and strategies into simple phrases, such as "the faceless opponent" and "every game is the Super Bowl."

In his 2011 Coach of the Year talk, Kelly said:

> "When I took over at the University of Oregon, the first thing we had to find out was "What do we stand for?" ... People should be able to come, observe you, and in five minutes know what you stand for."[12]

So what did Kelly's Ducks stand for? He boiled it down to four words:

Fast.

Work Hard.

Finish.

That's it. And if you've watched the Ducks over the last four years, that's exactly what you saw.

Oregon's football team is perhaps best known for its speed, both the quickness of its individual players—several of whom also run for Oregon's very successful track team—and the blitzkrieg pace of the Ducks' no-huddle offense. In the 2013 Fiesta Bowl against fifth-ranked Kansas State, Oregon scored eight points in the first twelve seconds of the game.

Hard work, as seen in Chip's rigorous and innovative approach to conditioning and practices, already has received a lot of attention in Philadelphia, and this book has a whole section devoted to the subject. Kelly's teams expect to be better conditioned and better trained than their opponents, and the Ducks outscored opponents dramatically in the fourth quarters of their games as a result.

But everything boils down to results. Finishing. One of the best measures of this goal is red zone scoring percentage—how often does a team score once they get inside their opponent's twenty-yard line? Since that is within field goal range for most kickers, the expectation is that they should score most of the time. By this measure, the Oregon Ducks excelled on both offense and defense.

In 2012, the Ducks scored on 90.77 percent of their red zone possessions, eighth best in the nation. In fact, the reality is even better than the number because Oregon rarely kicks field goals, so the team was scoring seven points where many teams settled for three. But the Ducks' red zone defense was just as good—69.39 percent, ninth best in the U.S.[13] Oregon's defense has never received the publicity that its offense does, but the Ducks led the nation with 131 takeaways during 2009-2012.[14]

Coach Kelly's vision for the Philadelphia Eagles will be different. He always adapts to the situation and the team. But you can be sure that he will have a clear statement of what they stand for and that it will be apparent to everyone. Not from words but from actions.

Players aren't impressed by a lot of talk and motivational speeches. Your concepts need to be translated into reality, which starts with practices. In that 2011 Coach of the Year talk, Kelly said:

"If a coach tells me respect is an important part of his program, I should see it in practice. If I go to practice and I see a player who takes a cheap shot at another player and no one corrects him, that program has no respect in it."[15]

Coaches lead best by example, and Kelly holds himself to the same standard: facts on the ground.

CHAPTER 3
WE FOCUS ON WHAT WE CAN CONTROL

Traditional football is seen as a chess match between the coaches. This can be true if both coaches stifle players' creativity and impose rigid plays and schemes on both sides of the ball. Then it's all about the coaches' cleverness and their battle of wills—a lot of ego for the guy in charge.

But one of those coaches always loses, and it's largely out of his control. A missed kick, a terrible call, a penalty, a bad bounce, or an opposing coach with a better chess move—any of these things can beat you, and there's nothing you can do about it. You can't predict these breaks, and your team won't be prepared to adjust.

Schemes and play calls don't win games. Execution wins games. You want a game plan that confuses your opponent, but if it also confuses your own players, you will lose.

The details of Chip's game plan for any given opponent are less important than his underlying philosophy, one that can be applied to any office or work team.

Get the best people available to you (for Chip, this means big and fast).

Build your strategy around those individuals.

Get them in top condition.

Make it easy for them to execute the strategy (through clear communication and diligent practice).

Force your opponent to show their plan as soon as possible.

Keep your plan hidden—or even undefined—as late as possible.

Execute.

That's it. Everything boils down to execution, so every part of your operation should aim toward improving execution. If a defender knows where the running back is going but can't get there in time, it doesn't matter what his coach tells him. You can have the most brilliant plan in the world, but if it requires talent you can't get, what's the point? On the other hand, if you have fast players performing at the top of their ability, it's going to be hard for your opponent to stop you even with a copy of your playbook. If you're really fast, like De'Anthony Thomas fast, it only takes one or two missed tackles before you score.

Start with reality, not with your grand schemes. Who is on your team? What is their maximum capability? All your coaching should be aimed at getting these individuals to their peak. And when you get new people, your brilliant plans should adapt. This de-emphasizes the coach's personal role, but it gets him more wins. The leader needs to swallow a little ego in order to succeed.

Cleverness is the enemy of execution. Thinking is way too slow to work at the highest levels of performance. Players need to stop thinking and react, using finely honed instincts developed through experience. That's why Kelly's teams emphasize running a lot of plays in practice. Not a lot of different plays—a lot of repetitions of the same plays, until running them becomes as automatic as driving your car to work.

As he said in his 2009 Coach of the Year talk,

> "With our inside zone play, we get so much practice time and so many reps that we can handle all the other scenarios that come about. Instead of trying to 'out-scheme' your opponent, put your players in an environment where they can be successful because they understand exactly what they have to do."[16]

Once again, the emphasis is on the players. The coach's role is to put *them* in a position to win.

CHAPTER 4
FEED THE TUNA MAYONNAISE

In 2009, George Schroeder—a reporter for the Eugene, Oregon *Register-Guard*—shadowed Kelly for a feature story about a (long) day in the life of the then-new coach.[17] Kelly worked endless hours, like most football coaches, but he didn't slack or give himself excuses for goofing off because of that, as many people who work long days do. Instead, Schroeder observed, Chip made it his mission "to find ways to squeeze more productivity from every minute of every very long day."

At one point, then-assistant coach Mark Helfrich showed up a bit late. Why? Because the bagel store he goes to was out of peanut butter. So Helfrich went to the supermarket to get some. Kelly's response? He said, "You had to get off the freeway? That's inefficient." In this case, it's hard to imagine what Helfrich could have done better—have an emergency ration of peanut butter standing by in his trunk?—but the point is, Chip is relentlessly looking for ways to cut the fat. His motto, he told Schroeder, is "Feed the tuna mayonnaise."

What the hell does that mean? With typically goofy humor, Kelly used a scene from the 1982 movie "Night Shift" to make fun of his own obsession with productivity. In that dark comedy, Michael Keaton plays a character who finds a way to make his underutilized workplace—a funeral home—more efficient by scheduling a different (if disreputable) business there at night. In a key scene, he has a sudden revelation about how to be more efficient, using the example of tuna fish. To make a tuna sandwich, you always have to mix it with mayonnaise.

Keaton, talking to himself and into a tape recorder, says "What if you mix the mayonnaise in the can, WITH the tuna fish? Or ... I got it! Take LIVE tuna fish, and feed 'em mayonnaise! Oh, this is great."

Chip likes film analogies. He told Chris Dufresne of the *Los Angeles Times* that if he had been the director of *Gone With the Wind*,

> "It would have been really fast. Get right to Atlanta, burn the buildings and yell 'Time!'"[18]

Apparently, though, he's not a foreign art film kind of guy. During a 2011 press conference, he said to a reporter:

> "C'mon, you've never seen *Fletch*?! WOW!!! It's a great movie!"[19]

But Kelly's focus on efficiency is no joke. His practices are broken into short, alternating periods of teaching and running plays, with pounding music pushing the tempo. No one stops to explain things to one player while everyone else stands around watching. If an individual needs instruction, he is substituted out of the plays until he gets it, while everyone else continues.

The goal is to run plays in practice not just as fast as during games, but faster. Players say that games seem easy and slow by comparison—which is a great feeling to have during a big game.

There are only eleven players on the field at a time, eleven weapons for a coach to use. You get the feeling that it kills this coach to see one of these eleven adding nothing to a play except acting as a decoy—like a wooden duck. Traditional NFL offenses line up two, three, or four receivers, and if the ball isn't thrown to them, they just slow down and return to the huddle. That's as many as four of your eleven, unproductive on every running play.

At Oregon, wide receivers were prized—and chosen— as much for their ability to block downfield on run plays and screens as for their pass catching. This was especially important because the Ducks were a run-first offense; they passed only one third of the time, something likely to change for Kelly in the pass-heavy NFL. Still, he is always looking to improve efficiency. One reason Oregon broke so many thirty-, forty- and fifty-yard runs was that receivers cleared out linebackers and safeties, extending an eight-to twelve-yard run into the kind of yardage most teams only get on passes.

All of Kelly's receivers block when they're not receiving, both downfield after runs and short passes and close to the line of scrimmage on wide runs. His running backs keep going into the flat when they don't have the ball, available for short "check down" passes—and for downfield blocking, just like receivers.

Defenders shift positions to cover injuries or adapt to different situations, and stars play on special teams. In 2012, Oregon's speedy slot back De'Anthony Thomas ran, caught passes, ran back punts and kickoffs (such as his touchdown that stunned Kansas State eight seconds into the Fiesta Bowl) and even served as a gunner on Oregon's rare punts.

Against Arizona State in 2012, Oregon had the ball, third-and-goal from the ASU two-yard line. Backup quarterback Bryan Bennett came in for a QB run sweeping to the left. (Running was Bennett's strongest suit, and the likelihood of a big hit on the play made the backup QB the logical choice to run it.) Bennett rolled left, but two linebackers grabbed him at the line of scrimmage. He then managed to wriggle out a little pass, almost like a Kareem Abdul-Jabbar skyhook, to the sideline—where starting quarterback Marcus Mariota caught it and ran in for a touchdown.

This wasn't a trick play, like some kind of halfback pass or flea-flicker. It was designed as a run, with the short pass as a backup option. Because his second string QB took the snap, Chip suddenly had a six foot four, 195-pound wide receiver who runs a 4.4 forty-yard dash available in Mariota. There was no way the coach was going to leave a wide receiver with perfect size and speed on the bench when he could improve the chances of getting that touchdown, even just a little. And this relentless focus on using all of his assets paid off with a TD.

Kelly's obsession with efficiency quickly made itself felt in Philadelphia. With a pro roster of only fifty-three players, compared to the 105 allowed to practice in college, efficiency is even more important, and it's all there—the blaring music, rapid-fire reps, even jogging from one weight machine to the next.

Players have noticed. Tight end Brent Celek told *Sports Illustrated*:

> "Everything is up-tempo now. It's go, go, go, go, go. All the time. But it's very efficient. We didn't know what to expect until we had that first practice and saw it, and it was a shock to your system. But I think probably almost everyone already has bought in. From the look at practice, guys are excited."[20]

Some of Coach Kelly's first practices with the Eagles involved drills where all five quarterbacks on the roster were standing in a row, throwing simultaneously to five receivers running five different routes, wave after wave.

It's just another way that Kelly feeds his tuna mayonnaise.

CHAPTER 5
THE BEST OF OUR ABILITIES
IS DEPENDABILITY

Football is highly unpredictable, especially at the college level. Teams rely on eighteen- to twenty-two-year-olds, most living away from home for the first time in their lives, heads swelled by fame and turned by every temptation life can offer.

So what do the colleges do? They put those kids in front of eighty thousand screaming fans and national TV cameras with huge emotional stakes and a career potentially worth millions of dollars on the line. I'm surprised that players don't have nervous breakdowns weekly.

Add to that the losses a team inevitably will suffer from graduation; injuries; alcohol, drug, and driving violations; and even more serious crimes, and you can see how hard it is to be consistently good. Whatever personnel difficulties you face at *your* job, they are almost certainly easier to handle.

Take the Auburn University Tigers, for example. They beat Oregon (narrowly) to win the 2010 National Championship Game. Two years later, their record was 3-9 and coach Gene Chizik was fired after just his fourth year, despite his championship ring.

Given these complications, Chip Kelly's consistency is at least as impressive as his 46-7 winning record. And it's not as though the Ducks lacked turmoil during his tenure. In his first three years as coach, Chip had to play nine different quarterbacks, and his team did well throughout, despite the unusual demands that Oregon's offense puts on a QB.

Early on, the Ducks lost linchpin players (such as quarterbacks Dennis Dixon and Jeremiah Masoli, All-American cornerback Cliff Harris, and running back LeGarrette Blount) to injury, legal troubles, and suspension for punching an opponent, respectively.

The character-related losses dwindled as players that Chip recruited filled the team, but injuries actually got worse. In the 2012-13 season, Oregon lost two key senior starters (offensive guard Carson York and safety John Boyett) by the second game.

The Ducks handled those key losses remarkably well. By the California game in mid-November, the Ducks were missing four starting defensive linemen plus star defensive end Dion Jordan, and in the middle of the game, Boyett's replacement, Avery Patterson, was also lost with a season-ending knee injury. This was a tough blow and a factor in Oregon's only loss, to Stanford, the following week—on a field goal in overtime.

Nonetheless, the Ducks weathered all these wounds and still went on to win the Fiesta Bowl and end the season ranked number two in the nation.

A similar string of injuries occurred during Kelly's first season in Philadelphia, during which Kelly was heard to say that "The best ability is durability." With starting second wide receiver Jeremy Maclin absent all year due to a knee injury and starting quarterback Michael Vick out with a hamstring, four more starters were out, injured by the end of the Eagles' tenth game, at Green Bay. (The Packers had their own injury problems.)

Yet even with the much smaller NFL roster, Kelly's substitutes at key positions, including quarterback, left tackle, safety, and inside linebacker stepped up and made the losses unnoticeable. Philadelphia won, 27-13, to move into a tie for first place in the NFC East division.

There are many ways that Kelly's programs build consistency. In particular, the clarity of vision, selection of versatile players, development of the depth chart, emphasis on conditioning, and delegation of control to players combine to give his teams a resilience and ability to adapt to any situation.

Chapter 6
Science Over Tradition

Football is a very conservative, traditional sport. A lot of things are done because "that's how it's done, what are you, some kind of fruitcake?" And Chip Kelly is having none of it. To him, that kind of thinking is just an opportunity for him to move ahead of his opponents, using the latest findings about nutrition, sleep, and conditioning.

In Philadelphia, the change is especially noticeable. In some ways, Kelly's predecessor, Andy Reid, was not so much traditional as actively anti-science. I know that sounds extreme but consider this: Reid actually had "Fast Food Fridays" and "Taco Tuesdays" for players in the Eagles' dining hall, while Kelly has replaced those with personalized smoothies for players, featuring healthy ingredients such as protein powder, blueberries, and peanut butter.

Reid's embrace of junk food, and the press' love of chattering about Chip's SCIENCE smacks of a *Revenge of the Nerds* mentality, pitting the big, bad, good ol' boys against scrawny science geeks. To my eye, this stereotype misses the point.

Chip Kelly is focused on results. He's not a Carl-Sagan-loving, quantum physics geek pursuing science for science's sake. He's looking for what has been proven to work. The scientific method is just another name for trying things and seeing what works. And that is his method to a T.

It's basic common sense, as Chip explained at the annual NFL owners' meeting:

> "Those are resources that are available to everybody. We're trying to put our guys in a position to be successful, so why not rely on what the experts say

is the right thing to do or wrong thing to do? ...

"Everybody has a dining hall, and they're not eating Tastykakes and Chickie and Pete's fries every night. When you get to this level, you are always talking about nutrition and their diet and things like that. Some guys do it and some guys leave the building and go to McDonald's. Did you get the right guy who is going to buy into what you're doing?"[21]

Granted, Chip pushes these issues further than anyone else and doesn't appear too worried about looking silly. He has opinions on how much water a player should drink and how much sleep they should get: "An elite athlete needs between ten and twelve hours a night." Brandon Graham, the Eagles 25-year-old linebacker, told Tim McManus of Birds 24/7 that the coach even asked him to wear a monitor on his wrist at night, to track how efficiently he is sleeping.

Oregon's college kids bought into all of this, but at a certain point the coach may lose some of his more jaded professional players (some as old as—gasp!—30). Perhaps he already has.

If so, this will be more evidence for Kelly to evaluate; will the more open-minded players who try these techniques outperform the attitude cases who will eat cheesesteaks if they damn well please?

If not, Chip will probably admit his mistake and backtrack, based on results. But it's hard to bet against good nutrition and sleep.

For now, anyway, Graham seems to be on board. He even hired his own nutritionist independently. Brandon told McManus:

"I see my body changing a lot. I really didn't know how dehydrated I was until they started doing that [sports science]. Now I'm hydrated, I'm moving a lot better out there, recovering a lot faster."[22]

Players may just be playing along with the new coach, but

even so, they'll find out if it works. And if it does work, any player with a decent attitude will get on board. Competition for NFL roster slots is fierce, and the pay is pretty good. If someone is willing to risk all of that for the sake of "Don't tell ME what to do!" they don't belong in the NFL anyway.

CHAPTER 7
WE'RE VERY, VERY FOCUSED ON THE PROCESS

In August 2012, just before he began his last season at Oregon, Chip Kelly told *USA Today*:

> "We're not an end-result operation. Our whole deal, why we're good, is because we're very, very focused on the process. ... If you come here, you'd better enjoy the process. It's not an end-result game. And if it is, then maybe this isn't the place for you."[23]

Wait—doesn't that contradict everything we've just established about Kelly's focus on results? Sure. It's a paradox, and Chip seems OK with that. On a deeper level, though, the paradox resolves itself. Good results come from following the process. Winning each day in practice leads to winning games.

There is also a difference between what coaches do and what players do. Chip's job is to see the big picture, to find an approach that generates good results. He is the one who evaluates what works, testing methods against outcomes and changing the plans accordingly.

Players don't need to see the big picture, and they should trust their coach to tell them what to do. He will. If anything, Kelly is relatively inclusive, making a point of telling players why they do everything they do, and that is one reason why nearly all of his players have climbed on board. But the players can and should stay in the moment.

"Focusing on the process" is just another way of saying "winning the day."

PERSONNEL

CHAPTER 8
OUR PROGRAM'S FOUNDED
ON COMPETITION

Practically from the moment he arrived in Philadelphia, the Eagles' new coach (and many of his players) were hounded by questions from reporters about the starting quarterback position. Will it be Michael Vick? Nick Foles? Matt Barkley? Dennis Dixon? (No offense to G.J. Kinne, who the Eagles snatched away from the San Antonio Talons of the Arena Football League,[24] but no one asked if it would be him.)

Apparently these reporters have not read up on Chip's years with the Oregon Ducks or listened to his somewhat patient answers to their endlessly repeated questions. Chip Kelly has open competitions for playing time. Period. I can repeat that if necessary—Chip Kelly has open competitions for playing time.

The number of reps (plays) you get to play during games is based on results. Results in practice, results in mini-camps, results in organized team activities (a.k.a. OTAs, the non-contact early workouts), results in the preseason. If you win a lot of days, you will win playing time during the regular season.

This may seem harsh to players who won starting roles the previous year and have to compete again, but the process is open and remarkably objective. Coach Kelly's programs go to extremes to maximize the number of reps run during practices, and his staff videotapes everything. How you perform in those plays—and how much you improve over the off-season—are the only things that matter when playing time is determined. What could be fairer?

On college signing day, 2012, he told a press conference that:

"I don't think we've ever had any kid complain that 'I don't get enough reps.' I think at the tempo and pace that we play at, that everyone gets a chance to show themselves on tape."[25]

No one is guaranteed playing time. How committed is Chip Kelly to this concept? Consider the case of Oregon quarterback Darron Thomas, which I wrote about for Bleeding Green Nation, the popular Philadelphia Eagles website.[26]

If his name doesn't ring a bell, well, frankly, it shouldn't for NFL fans. Following two amazing years at Oregon, Thomas went pro after his junior year, in the spring of 2012. "He didn't get a sniff from NFL teams," Charles Fischer of FishDuck.com told me. Darron's pro career to date consists of signing with the Calgary Stampeders of the Canadian Football League—for their practice squad.

Oregon fans were mystified why Thomas even considered going pro early—until they saw Marcus Mariota play the following season. The redshirt freshman was chosen as the PAC-12's first team all-conference quarterback—ahead of a USC player named Matt Barkley.[27] He was seventh in the nation in passing efficiency and led Oregon to a Fiesta Bowl victory over Kansas State and the number two AP ranking.

But hang on—Darron Thomas led the Ducks to the National Championship Game in his sophomore year, throwing for 363 yards and two touchdowns against Nick Fairley's Auburn in a last-second loss, and set Oregon's all-time record for career touchdowns with sixty-six. Isn't that enough to guarantee someone the starting job? Not on a Chip Kelly team. May the best man win.

In retrospect, it looks like Darron Thomas saw two tough quarterbacks ready to fight for his job: his backup, Bryan Bennett (who had played well in a couple games when Thomas was injured), and Mariota. Most likely Thomas decided to go pro before he could be benched. His odds of making an NFL roster may have been slim, but they were better as a successful junior starter than as a guy who got benched his senior year.

Kelly is bringing this same open attitude to Philadelphia. One of his first moves with the Eagles was to pay $4 million in guaranteed money to get rid of Nnamdi Asomugha, one of the highest-paid stars on the Eagles, without even seeing him in practice. Apparently last year's disastrous performance was evidence enough: a 120.6 passer rating on throws sent his way, according to Pro Football Focus[28]—the worst for any starting cornerback in the NFL—and an attitude that extended to regularly eating his lunch in his luxury car, away from teammates, for some "me time."[29] (After the Eagles released him, Nnamdi was signed as a free agent by the San Francisco 49ers for $1.35 million—more than 90 percent less than the $15 million he was scheduled to earn with the Eagles. They waived him after 8 games.)

Asked whether he felt that he needed to play Eagles lineman Danny Watkins because Watkins was a recent first-round pick, the coach reiterated:

> "I have no expectations of anybody. When I got here on January 16, it didn't matter to me if you were a first-round pick or an undrafted free agent. It's about putting the best team on the field. Where they got picked in the past or those things, it was a clean slate with us coming in."[30]

As we've already seen, Kelly designs practices that maximize the number of play repetitions—often more than one hundred reps in a two-and-a-half hour practice. One benefit is that this gives you a lot of objective data about performance. Chip Kelly's staff videotapes all of it and pores over the video in making personnel decisions. The offense plays against the defense constantly, and both sides know what's coming.

It all boils down to execution. It doesn't really matter how you did in the past, how famous you are, or what the coaches think you'll be able to do. Kelly designs training camps and practices that let him simply watch right now and see how you are doing. That and your improvement throughout camp are ultimately the only factors that matter. As Eagles QB coach Bill

Lazor said, when asked about the quarterback competition:

> "It's always best when it plays out on the field.
> When it plays out on the field, everyone sees it.
> Not everyone always agrees, but it plays out."[31]

Ideally the real world experience on the field makes it clear to everyone who the starter is. The coach doesn't even need to announce a decision; it's a fact right in front of everybody, and everyone knows. Offensive coordinator Pat Shurmur is on the same page.

> "Again, we've got a lot of training sessions left.
> We've got a full preseason, four preseason games.
> I think as we go through it and we add more and more to what we're doing; we're hopeful it'll be obvious to everyone who the starter is."[32]

This is part of Kelly's leadership: make it clear what the team is trying to do, then just do it, over and over, in practice and in games. When your goals are clear and everyone is working together, the starter is not chosen by the coach. There is no decision of his to criticize.

The choice is made by the players themselves, by what they do, or don't do, in the preseason. At Oregon, the 2012 spring game made it clear to everyone that Mariota deserved to be the starting quarterback over the much more experienced (and also very talented) Bennett. Mariota just got the job done.

CHAPTER 9
A QUARTERBACK IS LIKE A TEA BAG

Asked about how a new quarterback might do, Chip Kelly paraphrased Eleanor Roosevelt's famous quip about women:

> "They are like a tea bag. You don't know what you are going to get until you put them in hot water."[33]

He could have just as easily quoted Ronald Reagan when the former president said, "Trust but verify." Reagan was talking about arms control agreements with the Soviet Union right before that empire disintegrated, and it's questionable how much he ever trusted the Soviets, but that phrase is a great description of the way Kelly handles players and assistant coaches.

The coach is extremely diligent and hardworking, but he's not a micromanager or a control freak. He gives his players and coaches an extraordinary amount of freedom and control in their jobs and trusts them sincerely. Players make reads and can change the plan on the fly, not just the QB but also running backs and wide receivers (on option routes). In Philadelphia, Kelly's not even reserving play calls to himself—the assistant coaches are signaling the calls directly to their position players (a technique Kelly picked up from the University of Missouri).[34]

At the same time, results matter. Results verify (or falsify) whether you belong in your job, and videotape is an essential tool for Kelly.

This results-based decision making is similar to recent trends in business management, with one important difference: there is no fixation on quantitative measurements. No one is wasting time deriving statistics based on the video. The plays are right there, objective, and everyone can see them. The players know who executed and who didn't. The coaches know. And if anyone forgets, they can play it back.

Video also has one underappreciated advantage over statistical measures. It's a much richer data medium, even if it can't be dragged and dropped onto a spreadsheet. Every statistic is a drastic reduction of information, picking out one aspect of a complex reality and implicitly declaring that this one aspect is the most important thing to focus on.

In reality, of course, the statistic might not be the most important factor at all. It might just be the easiest thing to measure or something that a manager used at a previous job and is familiar with. It might reflect a subtle bias or a major assumption about how your business works. It can even be directly manipulated by an unscrupulous employee who picks a number that distorts results or builds up their numbers with methods that damage the business in the long run.

Luckily sports teams were among the first to recognize the limits of statistics. Every basketball fan has seen players that lead their team in scoring while neglecting defense and teamwork. It's possible to keep refining statistics and making them more elaborate to avoid this type of distortion, but the most data-rich medium will always be better for an attentive coach.

For Chip Kelly's teams, time of possession is a perfect example of a distorting statistic. Football coaches have emphasized this statistic for years. It gives them a sense of control, and in certain types of football games, this is accurate.

With their lightning quick attack, however, the Ducks invariably had less time of possession than their opponents. When most of your scoring drives take fewer than two minutes, how could it be any other way? All things being equal, a tie game with Oregon means you have had much more time of possession, just because it takes you longer to score. However, you're still tied, and as you get deep into the fourth quarter, that statistic favors the Ducks because they can always score quickly. A two-minute offense is actually slower than the Ducks' normal pace.

Furthermore, all things aren't equal. During Kelly's four

years at Oregon, the Ducks led the nation in takeaways. So the reality was, you drive for five minutes, lose the ball on a fumble or interception, and then the Ducks score in seventy-five seconds. How much is your time of possession advantage helping you now?

This reached an extreme in the 2013 Fiesta Bowl. Oregon's De'Anthony Thomas ran the opening kickoff back ninety-four yards for a touchdown, and the Ducks ran a quick two-point conversion past the stunned Kansas State Wildcats, who only managed to get nine defenders on the field. KSU had the ball back twelve seconds into the game—but they were down 8-0. "There's your time of possession right there," laughed TV analyst Todd Blackledge of ESPN.

As Kelly likes to say, the only statistic that matters is the number of points on the board at the end of the game. Many of his combative interactions with the press at Oregon were stoked by endless questions about time of possession, even as his team was dominating the PAC-12. Reporters often seemed unable to grasp that this statistic gives you no advantage at all against the Ducks.

In November of 2012, one reporter just couldn't let go of the time of possession question. Chip smiled, laughed, and tried to shrug off the persistent questions. Finally he gave this example:

> "Two years ago, a Thursday night game, we played UCLA. They ran seventy-three snaps, we ran seventy-one snaps. They had the ball for forty minutes, we had the ball for twenty minutes. We won 60-13."[35]

'Nuff said.

CHAPTER 10
BIG PEOPLE BEAT UP LITTLE PEOPLE

One of Kelly's wisest sayings came at the NFL's annual meeting press conference. A reporter asked why the Eagles were looking to get taller, longer players. He answered, simply,

> "We want taller, longer people because big people beat up little people."[36]

Besides the obvious truth of this statement, there is a more subtle message: don't outsmart yourself. Bright coaches such as Andy Reid can talk themselves into drafting someone that everyone else missed. But maybe everyone else "missed" them for a good reason. Even if a smaller player has admirable abilities and a great attitude, small stature can be a problem, and many feel that it was for Reid's teams. Speaking more generally, Kelly warned that,

> "If you sign an entire class of overachievers, I guarantee your team is going to be really small … The overachieving nose guard is six foot and the overachieving wideout is five seven and next thing you know, you're not gonna match up physically."[37]

One effect of not matching up physically is a lot of injuries, a problem that both Andy Reid's Eagles and Chip Kelly's Ducks faced. Those injuries were concentrated on the offensive and defensive lines, respectively, where size matters most.

At the same time, size doesn't always win. Oregon is a small school from a small state, and the University of New Hampshire was even smaller. Kelly has always had to make do against bigger opponents. During his first three years, the Ducks only had seven players drafted by the NFL; conference rivals Stanford and USC had eleven and nineteen draftees respectively.[38] Yet Oregon won two of its three games against each school.

That's in part because Chip developed lots of ways to work around his team's lack of size. At Oregon, which has had a nationally ranked track team since Steve Prefontaine's heyday in the 1970s, one obvious answer was speed. Another was conditioning, something a coach can control, and players who aren't five-star recruits may be easier to push toward fitness.

Yet another answer is treachery, such as the "Sucker Play," described by Charles Fischer at FishDuck.[39] The Sucker Play is not a bet designed for fools but rather a running play Oregon used in 2012 in their 62-point annihilation of the USC defense. (That game led defensive coordinator Monte Kiffin, a football legend who invented the Tampa-2 defense, to quit and take a job with the Dallas Cowboys as penance, though his feckless son Lane didn't take the hint.)

The Sucker Play is a trap, a misdirection running play where you "pull" a guard or tackle in one direction and run the other way. In a standard running play, an offensive lineman aims to push a defender back and to the side, creating a hole for the running back to burst through. Sometimes, in a "power play," a lineman steps back and runs to the side ("pulls"), usually looking to clear the way for a runner to sweep toward the sideline on an end around. Naturally linebackers who see this move run in that direction, to try to stop the play.

In the Sucker Play, the lineman pulls and runs, say, to the left. With any luck, defenders follow. But the pulling lineman has also created a hole in the line, just by running away from his position, if he can get his opposite number to follow him. A quick enough running back can slash through *that* hole or sweep in the other direction. The lineman has "blocked" his opposing player without even touching him, in the same way that the quarterback "blocks" a linebacker or defensive end in a zone-read play simply by looking at him—and redirecting the action.

Chip Kelly didn't invent the Sucker Play; it's as old as the hills. Kansas City used it to beat the Minnesota Vikings and their frightening defense in Super Bowl IV, way back in 1970. In the first game where a coach was mic'ed for TV during the Super Bowl, Hank Stram called out "65 Toss Power Trap" against the overaggressive Viking defense, and Mike Garrett ran through a hole as big as a subway tunnel for the Chief's first touchdown. (It was also the first Super Bowl with a celebrity halftime show, starring Carol Channing, but the less said about that the better.)

The Sucker Play is, however, quintessential Chip Kelly—a form of gridiron jujitsu that uses a defense's strength and quickness against itself. At Oregon, Kelly almost always had smaller offensive and defensive lines, especially against recruiting powers such as USC, Stanford, and the entire SEC conference, so he had to use speed and treachery to compensate. Oregon had used the Power Play against USC for two years, so the Trojans were ready to bite.

As Fischer diagrams, Oregon not only pulled multiple linemen to the left but even had a lineman on the right side block his man *to the right*, even though that was the direction that Kenjon Barner was going to run. All of this misdirection led the Trojan linebackers to overreact and sprint left, allowing Barner to score a touchdown wide to the right.

Now, this play may not work for Kelly in the NFL. After all, running away from his blockers leaves the running back unprotected, and a back not as fast as De'Anthony Thomas—who went to the NCAA National Track Championships in spring 2013—facing a quicker, older, and wiser NFL linebacker may just get crushed. But the point is that Kelly is a master at setting the rhythm of his offense—and playing against that rhythm to confuse his opponents.

In the NFL, Kelly won't face the recruiting disadvantages he struggled with at Oregon, either. He will never mutter the words "65 Toss Power Trap," but you can be sure he'll find a way to use his opponents' strength, effort, and planning against them. And if he can make sure his team's bigger in the first place, some really good things will happen.

Chapter 11
Players, Not Positions

Football is very conservative. Things are done a certain way, with fixed positions and plays. But none of that has to be. It's based on tradition, previous experience, what people know and are used to. These traditions generally work well, and they make it easy to learn and explain football. But they also blind you to possibilities.

Football has very few fixed limits. You must have at least seven players on the line of scrimmage, and only the two on the outside are eligible receivers. The rest is pretty much up to you. For a long time, coaches have fallen prey to the temptation of overspecialization, sticking with the rigid, fixed positions everyone is familiar with. This is heightened because players train to fit those positions and are drafted for fitting their requirements physically. But this limits you in your choices and makes your strategy much easier to predict and scheme against.

Chip Kelly fights against this in two ways: redefining positions more flexibly, and seeking versatile players who can play more than one role or shift from one position to another. Asked about his multitalented players at Oregon, specifically Kenjon Barner, he said:

> "We call 'em 'Jokers.' Cause jokers are good with any suit, any deck. It can be any card for you."[40]

In a no-huddle offense, the defense can't substitute until the offense does or the clock is stopped. If you can reconfigure your offense with the same personnel, the defense can't change to a situational defensive formation (such as a nickel package). This is a great way to defeat overcoaching. (It also is one reason Chip

Kelly likes to run or throw screens: to keep the clock running.)

Flexibility also allows you to make fuller use of your players' size and skills. Both Brandon Blair (a six foot seven defensive tackle) and Dion Jordan (a six foot six tight end converted into a defensive end) caught passes for two-point conversions during the Chip years at Oregon, out of the unusual "swinging gate" formation. They both have the skills to play both offense and defense like some high school players do, though obviously no one can do that at the top level of college ball (especially at Chip Kelly's pace). But defensive coordinator Nick Aliotti could certainly share them for one play a game, especially if it gained Oregon an extra point.

In his efforts to break out of the limits of traditional positions, Kelly went so far as to invent a new one, dubbed the Tazer (or TAZR). Tazers can line up in the slot, in the backfield, or at any of the wide receiver positions. They were designed to make full use of Oregon's abundance of speedy runners who could catch passes, including Ed Dickson, LaMichael James, Kenjon Barner, and De'Anthony Thomas.

Dickson explained another advantage of Tazers to ESPN's Ted Miller.

> "We can freeze a guy in motion when we run our routes—that's why they call it a tazer. You taze somebody and they're stuck. That's what we do to somebody when we run our routes."[41]

Yet another advantage of this kind of flexibility is that you can draft great athletes and adapt them to your team's needs. Kenjon Barner was defensive back first and ended up as a star running back. Dion Jordan was a tight end and became a defensive end—drafted third overall in the 2013 NFL draft for his talent. In addition to finding the perfect fit, this gives you insurance against injuries, letting you move a player to fill a desperate need.

In his new NFL job, Kelly has already used the Eagles number four overall draft pick on Lane Johnson, a freakishly athletic six foot six offensive lineman who was an honorable mention all-state quarterback at his Texas high school, then started as a tight end at Oklahoma and shifted to right tackle. I wouldn't be surprised to see him catch or even throw a pass under Chip, particularly on an extra point conversion, though he'll have to notify the referee that he's becoming eligible before the play (or take the snap under center).

More generally, focusing on players rather than positions opens you up to a wider range of possibilities. Think of a piano. There are an infinite number of tones in any octave, but a piano forces you to use just twelve of them, the seven white and five black keys. It's much easier to write music for a piano or teach someone to play one, but you lose the ability to play all those other notes.

Chip Kelly has invented the football equivalent of an electric guitar, where he can play fixed notes but also bend the strings and get all those tones in between the piano keys. And when everyone is used to pianos, they forget about all of those other tones. There isn't a way to even write them down on your sheet music, but they haven't disappeared; everyone has just forgotten about them. Chip not only bends those strings, he cranks up the amplifier and plays with feedback like Jimi Hendrix.

CHAPTER 12
NEXT MAN IN

Managing injuries is one of the most difficult tasks for an NFL coach, due to small rosters, hard-hitting linebackers, and the irreplaceable talent of many stars. Not all of the methods that Kelly used in Oregon will apply to the Eagles, but many will. Coach Kelly is picking up versatile players (like fullback/tight end James Casey), cross-training them in practice, and drawing up schemes with flexible and overlapping positions.

One striking aspect of his game management is his active rotation of players down into the depth chart, especially on defense. Because of his teams' fast offensive drives, Chip's defenders are on the field a lot. With the Ducks, Kelly sometimes brought in a whole wave of substitutes, almost like a line shift in hockey. And whenever he has a large lead, he brings in second- and third-string players at various positions. (He'd probably do the same if his team were hopelessly behind, but we can't be sure because this literally has never happened in his 53 games as coach.)

This active substitution has several advantages. Obviously it keeps players fresh, which amplifies the conditioning advantage Kelly's teams already have. It helps develop talent further down on the depth chart and gives coaches a chance to see how those players perform in real game situations. And perhaps most importantly, it ensures that if injuries do happen, substitutes will be seasoned and ready, not feeling pressured by suddenly being in a game.

Of course, the Eagles won't be able to substitute the way that Oregon, with twice as many players on the roster, could. But the insurance against injuries will be that much more important for the same reason. Last year, the Eagles were decimated by injuries in large part because they lacked this flexibility to adjust. (Slack conditioning and "Fast Food Fridays" probably didn't help, either.)

Kelly also prepares his team mentally with yet another of his punchy mottoes: "Next Man In." The 2012-13 season was a perfect illustration. The year had begun with two devastating injuries to starters Carson York (an offensive lineman) and star safety John Boyett. Junior Avery Patterson had stepped up and done a great job replacing Boyett.

In their November 10 game against California, Oregon had an unbelievable run of additional injuries. Their top five defensive linemen were all out, including star defensive end Dion Jordan. Quarterback Marcus Mariota and star running back Kenjon Barner had to leave the game temporarily, wounded.

The final straw occurred when Avery Patterson, who had done so well stepping in for John Boyett, was lost for the season in the second quarter with an ACL tear. Kelly was asked if he felt bad for Patterson. Typically, he was philosophical.

> "When a player gets hurt, I feel for all of those guys. They've given their heart and soul to this program [but] you can't just sit there and feel sorry for him while the game's going on … I felt bad for John Boyett [too], … but if our mentality's not "Next Man In," then Avery wouldn't have played as well when *he* subbed, [when *he*] was next man in."[42]

It may seem cold or unsympathetic from the outside, but these are highly competitive players. Would they really feel honored by having their team deflate and lose in their absence?

Incidentally, Oregon won the game 59-17, though the injuries contributed to their narrow loss to Stanford in overtime the following week.

CHAPTER 13
WE HAVE SIXTEEN SQUAD LEADERS

One aspect of Chip Kelly's programs that has been overlooked is the way that he cultivates a certain egolessness in his teams and coaching staffs.

(That may be because he's supremely confident in his own approach, but Chip's confidence is earned. He's a blue collar guy who is smart, works harder than anybody else, and wins. It would be kind of weird, or unrealistic, if he weren't confident.)

He doesn't just prefer relatively humble team players as a way to keep the team cohesive; he cultivates them and builds this into the team's structure. This is done not by discouraging leadership but by encouraging *more* leadership so that there are many leaders on a team.

After the Ducks' first spring practice of 2011, he told a press conference:

> "There aren't many people that are born leaders, but you can cultivate that. Then just like you can teach them a scheme like run offensively or defensively, you can teach them how to be a really good leader."[43]

At Oregon, instead of having one or two team captains, they had sixteen—one leader for each position—and Kelly let the players choose who those leaders would be, because

> "… those guys have a better feeling for it. Once we have those sixteen squad leaders, I spend more time with those guys than anybody else. Talking about what being a leader is all about. Be the first to serve, be the last to be served. Be the first one

to identify what our team standards are and be the last to break them."

A key leadership task is building the allegiance of the people under you. This is even harder when you are breaking so many traditions and asking your team to innovate in unfamiliar ways. Many leaders (and parents) throughout history have noticed that a great way to get strong personalities to identify with them—and not rebel against them—is to put those people in a position of authority. If it turns out well, you've also developed their power as individuals in a way that benefits your team.

Kelly's programs have done this both with the players and with assistant coaches. In Philadelphia, plays will not just be called by the head coach and relayed in. Position coaches will be sending signals in to just their players, allowing much more specific and complicated messages and making it impossible for opponents to steal the calls in time to relay them to their players.

When you increase the number of leaders and train people for leadership, you build a team where someone is always ready to step up and take the initiative, not to increase their personal power and glory, but because the moment calls for it. That is a strong and resilient team.

CHAPTER 14
WE CELEBRATE AS A TEAM

Chip Kelly doesn't seem to like heroes much. A hero pulls your team from a loss to a win through some improbable clutch play, against all odds. That's a situation Kelly never wants to be in because heroes emerge when a team is struggling, and they make the victory all about them as an individual. He'd rather have a team that looks like the big bad bully and wins by thirty-two points with a group of unsung role players.

Kelly is a star coach who has had a succession of star players (LaMichael James, Kenjon Barner, De'Anthony Thomas, Marcus Mariota). And yet, his teams work hard to minimize individual ego and promote the team.

Many athletes pay lip service to this, mechanically thanking the offensive line for all their success, but at Oregon it goes deeper. In part, this is because Kelly's program makes individual stars less crucial, and minimizing egos makes a team more reliable.

> "We tell our guys one thing: When you score a touchdown, you celebrate as a team. Because you're not the only guy that got yourself in the end zone. If it's a receiver, then that means we had an offensive line blocking for you and gave the quarterback time."

One of the big questions about Kelly's move to the NFL is whether it's even possible to get NFL stars to play with humility and a team focus, especially with the Eagles, a team some wags have called "The Philadelphia Egos."

Part of the answer is, being part of a winning team is a

lot more fun than being a big shot on a squad that goes 4-12, as Philadelphia did in Andy Reid's last year as coach. Chip gets this, too.

> "We always want to celebrate as a team. That's a big thing for us, and if you watch our guys do it, I think they really get excited; whether it's a big play on defense or someone scoring a touchdown, there's a lot of guys getting around there and celebrating."[44]

PRACTICE

Chapter 15
The Only Proven Shortcut
to Success is Hard Work

Nothing is more distinctive in a Chip Kelly program than his practices, which are fast and uniquely structured into alternating short periods of teaching and running plays. Loud music blares throughout so that players get a taste of the excitement and confusion of a game and don't get used to communicating with their voice—which will be useless in game situations.

Everything is done to mirror the way Kelly wants his games to happen. The team runs as many plays as possible, routinely 135 or so, sometimes 150, which has a lot of advantages. In his 2012 Coach of the Year talk, Kelly said:

> "We do not condition at the end of practice. We condition during practice. In a twelve-minute period, we get thirty-six repetitions."

Players learn the complicated plays by muscle memory so that these plays are carried out by instinct during the game and don't require thinking. This increases both the speed and execution of plays dramatically.

The attitude of urgency even goes beyond full practices. Eagles players were surprised to hear that they should also lift weights faster and run to the next weight station.

Kelly also minimizes talking during practice. Instruction should be done, wherever possible, in a classroom or video session. Practices, which are limited in time by rules, should focus on actual play wherever possible. To maximize efficiency, some drills involve multiple players; in one drill, the Eagles had a row of five quarterbacks throwing to waves of five receivers at a time, running five different routes.

It's hard to overstate how important this hard work in practice is to the game-time power of Chip's teams, which rely on rhythm so much. One rhythm is that of an offense on a drive; it's crucial to establish your own rhythm on offense and disrupt that of your opponents on defense.

Then there are the broader rhythms, following the body's cycles (especially sleep) and the natural unit of football time—the week. Kelly's teams work backward from game time and game day (which shifts, especially in the NFL) so that hard workouts, run-throughs, and even meals are set a certain amount of time before kickoff. This is even more important in high-pressure games so that the familiarity of the routine settles players and gets them back into muscle memory, not in their heads.

When the Ducks were preparing for the National Championship Game, in Kelly's second season at Oregon, he told reporters:

> "It's a business trip. Our guys know we keep the same schedule—when we leave [campus], when we get to the airport, when it's wheels up. It's just like any other away game for us."[45]

It's also important, in a time when other teams are adopting no-huddle and zone-read strategies, that the defense gets crucial experience against this still-novel offense in their own practices.

> "We pride ourselves on our preparation. The three things we control is our preparation, our effort, and our attitude."[46]

This may all seem driven, extreme, perhaps a waste of energy better saved for game time. Yet the results are consistent—opponents suck wind, and Kelly's teams pull away from them in the fourth quarter, game after game. It makes more sense if you think of other areas of life. Would you want an expensive restaurant you ate at to take shortcuts? Kelly explained it this way to *USA Today*:

"I think we live in a microwave society. But I don't think anybody in this world would say, 'Hey, there's a brand-new microwave restaurant that opened up down the road. Let's go eat at it.' No one would want to go to it. They want to go to a place where they enjoy the process in the kitchen and they take a lot of time in preparing the food for you."[47]

Chapter 16
You've Got to Practice in It if
You're Going to Play in It

It's not just that players have to practice a play relentlessly before they try it during a real game. Kelly wants everything you do in practice to be as close as possible to the way you do it in a real game.

For seventeen years, the Eagles held their training camp at Lehigh College, a beautiful location not far from Philadelphia. Chip immediately moved it back to the Eagles' home field (Lincoln Financial Field) and the team's NovaCare Complex training facilities. That saddened a lot of people who enjoyed the tradition of the trip out to the country for camp, not to mention fans who lived near there.

But all of that is secondary to winning games. For Kelly, it's crucial that practices match game conditions as much as possible so that you're that much more prepared.

At one practice early in Kelly's Philly regime, it started raining. Reporters expected to move inside for the rest of practice, as had apparently happened under Andy Reid, and asked Chip why he didn't. Kelly noted that special teams can't practice fully indoors and added sarcastically:

> "I think football's played outside. Last time I checked, [Lincoln Financial Field] doesn't have a dome. It rained a little bit. I know it may have been a little inconvenient for you guys, and I do apologize for that, but I think we had a practice. It wasn't like we had a hurricane or anything like that."

Keep in mind that Kelly had just spent six years in Eugene, Oregon (two as the offensive coordinator and four as head coach). There's a reason that the University of Oregon named their team the Ducks; it rains very often, especially during football season. (Then again, NFL games are played in snow and subfreezing temperatures, too.)

Anyway, one reporter kept pushing Kelly about how Andy Reid would have found a way to move the practice inside. Finally, the coach said:

> "I don't know what went on in [Reid's] practice, but I know you've got to practice in it if you're going to play in it. We've always felt that. Unless it's just so bad that you can't be productive. But we had some guys slipping and sliding a little bit. They have to learn to stay on their feet in those situations, so we felt it was good working outside today."

The difficult conditions are not a problem here; they're a plus because they make the players more ready for whatever situation might arise in a game. Obviously a team with that experience will do better when they play in rainy conditions.

Practices are not always going to be exactly like a game. There aren't eighty thousand fans in the seats, for one thing. But Kelly plays blaring, high-energy music throughout practices. This has several interesting advantages. Most simply, it prevents you from hearing each other talk, just like games. It's a bad habit to get used to talking or yelling at your teammates, when opposing fans can disrupt that by hollering.

Other teams pump in white noise or static to simulate that sonic disruption. Not Chip. For one thing, it just annoys him. But it also deadens the emotion of the moment and is too uniform. By playing a crazy mixture of high energy dance, rock, hip-hop, and country music, the team simulates a bit of the excitement as well as the chaos of game day.

The goofiest game simulation that Kelly runs comes in early practices, before the pads come on. Teams typically run seven-on-seven scrimmages—in other words, without any linemen blocking because there's no contact yet at this point in the preseason.

That's still useful because the running backs and receivers run their routes against the defensive backs and linebackers. But it can lead to bad habits because the quarterback can throw a low pass that would easily be batted down or picked off in a real game by the missing linemen. Or even hit the offensive linemen in the back of their heads.

So Kelly has evolved a makeshift way to simulate the linebackers. Assistants put on backpacks with tall mesh flaps that rise up to six feet four inches, the size of a typical defensive lineman with his hands up.[48] Reporters usually call these "fly swatters," but they really look more like giant fly's wings made of black mesh or a very cheap sail on a low-quality windsurfing board.

Yes, it's goofy, but Kelly isn't worried about what people think of his practices. As long as his teams win games, people fall in line. The important point is not to develop bad habits while you're training. To do that, you have to force people to work just as hard in practice and follow all of the same standards, as they would in a real game.

CHAPTER 17
IF YOU ACCEPT IT, EXPECT IT

"You don't rise to the occasion; you sink to the level of your preparation."[49]

It's crucial in the Kelly system to catch bad habits in practice and break them there, long before game time. In the pressure and unpredictable flux of a game, you don't have time to analyze or think about what to do. You will react based on the instincts you developed in practice, so bad habits that are uncorrected are sure to re-emerge during a game. It's muscle memory, not intellectual thought, that drives your actions at game speed.

"It's amazing how when you don't have bad practices, you don't have bad games."[50]

This has been proven by recent research into the brain. It turns out that pathways in the brain actually reinforce themselves through use, so the concept of habits is not just a nagging point from your grandmother; it's a fact, burned into your brain through repetition.

The coach states this message as clearly as possible in his 2012 Coach of the Year lecture:

"If the player lines up two yards over the start line in sprints and you do not correct him, do not jump his butt when he does it in the game. ... If you do not correct the offensive lineman in practice for holding, do not bitch at the official for calling it in the game. If you accept it, you should expect it in the games, and that is on the coach."[51]

Chapter 18
Teach to the Fastest Learner

As Kelly took over in Philadelphia, a reporter asked him about the challenge of teaching entire new systems and schemes to a new team. His response was simple, and applies to every workplace:

> "You teach the fastest learner, and everyone else has to catch up."[52]

In school, every kid deserves to be taught, and teachers need to make sure that "no child is left behind" as best they can. But once you're building a competitive team or business, that philosophy is disastrous. It's not a charity, and you're not just accomplishing the task of communicating information. You're also creating a culture and an expectation for your team. You, as the coach or boss, are setting the tone beginning with the first minute of orientation. Do you demand the best and create a culture of excellence? Or do you accept mediocrity and let the weakest link define the strength of the chain?

Everyone says they want excellence, but few have the guts to get rid of people who are mediocre. No one enjoys that, but it's necessary. Of course, if you aren't careful to make your process fair, transparent, and results-based—to keep your ego and personal biases out of it—the ruthlessness quickly turns to petty politics and bad morale.

The sweet spot is a culture that moves fast and rewards hard work but shares a pride and camaraderie based on excelling together. That's what Chip achieved at Oregon. Once again, de-emphasizing his own role was part of the method. As he explained in his 2012 Coach of the Year lecture, learning is a three step process.

1. I SEE (OR HEAR) AND I FORGET.

By this, Coach Kelly is referring to teaching with words and diagrams—*telling* a student what to do. He estimates that only 5 percent of information delivered this way is retained and brings up a subtle point. When you say something like "cut at a 45 percent angle," the player forms a picture of what that means in his mind. But his picture might be very different than yours.

Abstraction is a very powerful tool for condensing and delivering knowledge. But it also opens up a lot of potential for miscommunication. Think of how many times you have heard the lyrics to a song and understood them to mean something very different than your friend does. That abstraction has some interesting uses, but it's a big liability in teaching specific physical techniques.

2. I SEE AND I REMEMBER.

This refers to seeing a skill actually demonstrated, on video or—better yet—by a teammate who gets it. The actual performance of a skill contains a much richer vein of information than the abstraction of words or diagrams depicting it.

3. I DO AND I UNDERSTAND.

People learn best by doing. It's that simple. First at "teach speed," a walk through, until they understand all the actions involved. Then at game speed, full bore ahead, running the play as many times in practice as possible until it's second nature.

Leadership begins with example, and Chip himself has always been the fastest and most insatiable learner as a player and as a coach. As a young assistant, his own fast learning impressed legendary University of New Hampshire coach Bill Bowes, a former offensive lineman, who reluctantly promoted Chip to offensive line coach.

> "I thought it best to hire someone who had played offensive line to coach it, [but] Chip talked me into it. To my amazement, he picked it up exceptionally fast. He was a young coach who wanted to know

everything about football."[53]

As he rose through the ranks at the University of New Hampshire, he paid his own way to view other football teams that pursued similar spread offense strategies, wherever they might be: NFL Europe and Canadian Football League teams abroad as well as US colleges and even high school teams whose success was spread along the grapevine.

Kelly's off-season travels took him to Georgia Tech, Wake Forest, Clemson, Northwestern, and Oregon—where his knowledge (and unquenchable thirst for more knowledge) caught the eye of coach Mike Bellotti.

Despite his success, Kelly has never stopped learning or wanting to learn. Just before the 2012 USC game (which Oregon won 62-51), Kelly told a reporter:

> "The area of improvement for everybody is everything. We'll never arrive. And that's the key … to think you never have arrived."[54]

CHAPTER 19
WATER THE BAMBOO

Chip got this idea from Greg Bell, a motivational speaker and business consultant who used to play basketball for the University of Oregon. Bell starts with a great metaphor about hard work.

There's a species of bamboo that has an unusual growth pattern, the Giant Timber Bamboo. (What else would you expect from an Oregon author?) Chip put it this way after the 2009 Oregon State game:

> "If you water [this type of] bamboo in the first year, nothing happens. If you water it in the second year, nothing happens. If you water it in the third year, nothing happens. If you water it in the fourth year, it grows ninety feet in six weeks."[55]

The meaning is pretty clear, even if you don't coach at a four year college. Whatever it is that you do, you have to keep working hard, for years even, without worrying about the lack of visible results, because you're building strength ("strong and resilient roots," as Bell puts it) that will pay off in the long run.

Chip explains it this way:

> "Whether it's life or whether it's football, you just gotta keep watering the bamboo and eventually it'll grow for you."[56]

STRATEGY

CHAPTER 20
WE DON'T RUN SOME MAGICAL OFFENSE OR DEFENSE

The offensive records that his teams keep breaking lead some writers to imagine that Kelly delivers an onslaught of tricky plays, and that his teams pass a lot. How else could they average forty-eight points a game?!

He's a great innovator, but Chip Kelly never loses touch with football fundamentals—or with common sense. Much of his football is very traditional, just MORE—more practice, more flexibility, more speed, more conditioning. In many ways, he aims to de-emphasize the importance of his play-calling and seek every other kind of advantage, especially in better execution of his game plans (whatever they are).

When all is said and done, Kelly's teams just run the ball a lot. There's nothing more traditional than that. (It's also crucial to the full-speed, no-huddle offense because if the clock doesn't stop, the defense is not allowed to substitute. Every incomplete pass or sideline receiver pushed out of bounds throws away this advantage.)

Just as importantly, the coach understands that keeping your offense simple is itself a big advantage. It helps players learn, execute, and perform much more quickly.

The strategy is very simple. Use the spread formation to force your opponent to show their plans as early as possible and keep yours hidden as late as possible. If at all possible, let your skill players decide what to do after they see the defense's choices, before or even after the snap. This is the goal of the zone-read play, and if you can execute it properly, it's devastating.

A well-played zone read is like a game of rock, paper,

scissors where you get to throw your hand sign one second after your opponent throws theirs. You can see what the winning move is and simply do it. The only reason you would lose is if you throw the wrong sign by accident.

The most effective way for a defense to stop the zone read is to take away that one-second advantage by masking their choice and not overcommitting to what the offense seems to be doing. This was the strategy Stanford used to defeat a beat-up Oregon squad in 2012, but it's easier said than done.

People who watched the Ducks over the past four years often made the mistake of thinking that the offense was much more complicated than it really is. In fact, when you are playing the no-huddle quickly, you have to keep it simple. You are pushing the defense to the limit of their ability to read your formation and line up correctly. If you get set up before they're ready, a very simple play can break for big yards, especially with fast skill players and downfield blocking to grab the most yardage possible.

Ultimately Kelly wants to force the defense to make a clear choice. And he has any answer for any choice they make. Asked about how he would juggle three talented tight ends on the Eagles' roster, he said:

> "We are going to go three tight ends in a game. Now, do they go three linebackers? We split them out and throw passes. If they go three DB's, we smash you [with running plays]. ... Simple game. Isn't hard. You guys thought coaching was hard. They bring little guys in, you run the ball. They bring big guys in, you throw the ball."[57]

It is simple. And nearly impossible to stop.

CHAPTER 21
EVERYTHING YOU DO HAS
TO BE PERSONNEL-DRIVEN

The most interesting paradox of Chip Kelly is that he has brilliant plays and schemes—which he is always changing and replacing. And he constantly downplays the importance of his strategies as opposed to the importance of his players.

This is not a contradiction, and he is absolutely right. The biggest mistake a coach can make is to think that he is playing. He's not. The players are.

Everything a coach does must serve the players and make them better. Chip calls this "putting them in a position to win." Because the *players* are the ones who win. That's why Kelly changes his strategies with each new group of players and why his plays themselves give players more control in the moment to make key choices; quarterback reads, receiver option routes, running backs with carte blanche to turn around and run the other way (and the quickness to pull that off) are all part of the system.

If a team's players can't execute some elaborate play or understand what the coach is talking about, that's not their error—it's the coach's.

Kelly also knows that elite players can disrupt even the best plans. His two bowl losses came largely at the hand of three extraordinary players: Terelle Pryor at Ohio State, in Kelly's first Rose Bowl, and Cam Newton and Nick Fairley from Auburn, in the National Championship Game.

Already NFL scouts are misreading Kelly's Eagles because they don't realize that his college coaching strategy related to having relatively small offensive and defensive lines at Oregon.

Going for it on fourth down? The Ducks had terrible field goal kicking, which arguably cost them two national championships (the loss to Auburn, clearly, and their overtime loss in 2012-13 to Stanford, 17-14, which kept Oregon out of the 2013 National Championship Game). As Chip said shortly after the Eagles hired him,

> "A lot of our decisions came in the kicking game. If you don't have a guy that can kick a long field goal, what are you going to do when the ball is on the thirty-seven yard line? Will you kick a fifty-two-yarder, or are you going to punt it? If it goes in the end zone, you have a net of seventeen yards. Or do you go for it because you have a good defense, and you're not averse to putting them on the field on the thirty-seven yard line? Those weren't statistical decisions."[58]

Kelly's adaptability is one of his signature qualities. In New Hampshire, with a great passing quarterback, his team set passing records.[59] At Oregon, he cycled through dual-threat quarterbacks, running quarterbacks, and relatively immobile quarterbacks—and won with all of them, shifting strategy to match.

It's not that your players limit your fabulous strategy. The strategy starts with the talent you have and emerges from that range of possibilities. In a press conference before the National Championship Game in 2011, Kelly said that:

> "[Play calling] is driven by the players that you have … you can't be a riverboat gambler if you are coaching the Little Giants."[60]

During the NFL Annual Meeting press conference, he said that this attitude was why he hired Billy Davis as his defensive coordinator.

> "You can say we want to run this defense, but if we don't have that personnel available to us, we would

still have to play games. So how do we adapt and what do we do to adjust? That's one of the great strengths of Billy's; he has that ability to adjust and adapt depending on what kind of personnel he has."[61]

There is a constant push in Chip's football programs to stay reality-based, to adapt to the situation. I guarantee you that if the players in the game called for a completely different offense, Kelly would throw away all of his innovations in a second without looking back.

CHAPTER 22
TAKE WHAT THE DEFENSE GIVES YOU

Many coaches urge their teams to take what the defense gives them, but few build their strategy around the concept. Chip Kelly does.

His fundamental strategy is to force the players on the opposing team to make difficult decisions under pressure. Kelly's teams are waiting with a simple plan to take advantage of whichever choice they make.

On offense, Kelly most prizes quarterbacks (and other skill players) who can quickly and decisively read the opponent. He will equip them with ways to punish any choice. A lot of elite quarterbacks make good pre-snap reads, but Chip teaches effective post-snap reads, most notably in read-option plays.

A pre-snap read can be defeated by disguising the defense, sending players up into the box who might blitz or fall back into coverage. But a post-snap read is not vulnerable to such trickery. It's difficult to execute, but that's what practice is for.

Chip Kelly is at the forefront of a major NFL trend toward "packaged plays," a much more sophisticated version of the old option play. In the option, the quarterback ran wide, with a choice to pass, keep the ball and run, or pitch to a running back. A package play might involve a quarterback who can hand off to the running back who's going left, or keep it himself to go right, or toss a quick screen to either sideline, or throw a pop pass up the seam to a tight end.

The defense can stop any one or two of these, but in doing so, they will leave at least one of the other choices under-defended. Not every quarterback can read the situation and make the perfect choice quickly enough, but those who can are very difficult to stop.

Chris Brown has written extensively about these plays for Grantland.com[62] and for his own website, Smart Football.[63]

Chip's packaged plays are surprisingly simple for the offense to run. The offensive line simply blocks for a run play, whatever the quarterback chooses—so he'd better get rid of the ball fast.

Even for the quarterback, the decision is relatively simple. He just needs to count the number of defenders in "the box" around the center. If they send an extra linebacker or safety up to stop the run, filling the box with seven or eight defenders, you throw. If they drop back and leave only six defenders in the box (the "nickel" defense with five backs) or, God willing, five defenders (the "dime"), you run. It's simple math.

The nickel defense, by the way, was invented by Philadelphia defensive backs coach Jerry Williams during the Eagles' 1960 championship season, to stop a star tight end for the Chicago Bears named Mike Ditka.

Which run? The read option leaves a defender unblocked, usually a defensive end, and sends the play where he does not go. If he crashes inside toward the running back, the quarterback keeps the ball and runs past him. If he hangs back to stop that, the running back should have a good crease up the middle.

There are some moving parts, certainly, but after a few hundred reps, a quarterback with a talent for reading the defense should react instinctively and find some relatively easy yards.

Best of all, there's not a lot of trickery here. It's one simple play that you can run over and over, with different results each time. And most of those results are very good.

CHAPTER 23
THE FACELESS OPPONENT

One of the most mysterious slogans Chip Kelly uses is "The Faceless Opponent," (sometimes expressed as "The Nameless Opponent"). Like "Win the Day!®," it incorporates several different meanings.

One meaning is the importance of using professionalism and execution instead of emotion to win games. A good game plan will—generally speaking—work the same against powerful teams and weaker teams. If your strategy only works against patsies, you should probably get a new one.

Coaches and teams can get caught up in second-guessing what the other team might do. Chip prefers to teach players—and design schemes—to recognize and adapt to whatever the other team does. Then you can focus on nailing down your scheme, and you control the outcome, whatever your opponent does.

When Kelly first led the Ducks against USC in 2009, few programs were as dominant as Pete Carroll's number-four-ranked Trojans, who had won seven straight PAC-10 championships in a row and picked up a few (now-disputed) national championships during that stretch. USC had not lost by more than a touchdown in eight years.

Oregon and its first-year coach were still smarting from the Boise State debacle in the first game of that season. Star running back LeGarrette Blount could not play, still suspended for punching a Broncos defensive end.

So what did the Ducks do, in their biggest high-pressure game of the year? They stuck to their usual game plan and focused on executing it. And they won, 47-20, USC's worst loss in eleven years. Oregon's offense dropped 613 yards on the

Trojans—the most they had given up since 1946.[64]

Jeremiah Masoli was asked if Oregon made a statement against the team widely declared to be the decade's dominant squad:

> "I don't know if we made a statement; this is just what we planned on doing. If it makes a statement, it makes a statement. That's just Oregon football and how we roll."[65]

That's how you beat a faceless opponent, by doing what you do as well as possible. Then it hardly matters who your opponent is. USC was a deeply talented and experienced team. They had scouted Oregon carefully and watched all of the video. They knew what was coming. They had planned for everything Oregon threw at them.

How did that work out for them? Ask Taylor Mays, that USC squad's hard-hitting and always quotable safety.

> "They just beat us up front; they just beat us up. They hit us in the mouth and kept hitting us in the mouth."[66]

CHAPTER 24
JUST TELL ME THE RULES OF THE
GAME AND I WILL PLAY BY THEM

Accepting and adapting to reality is a major part of Chip Kelly's philosophy. So is not getting uselessly emotional or angry, as so many coaches do.

In 2011, Stanford aimed to slow down the Duck's offense, not by faking injuries—as Cal had done the year before—but by letting the grass on their field grow long. It had rained recently, and the theory was that long, wet grass might mess up Oregon's quick offensive rhythm.

As it turns out, the gambit mostly helped the Ducks, and Kelly was wryly amused:

> "Yeah, I'm kind of surprised a school like this didn't have a lawn mower. But they had to play on the grass, too. A couple of their guys slipped and fell out there, including [quarterback Andrew] Luck."[67]

That maneuver ignored one obvious fact; it rains a lot more in Eugene than in Palo Alto, and it doesn't take a genius to guess who would adapt to a wet field better. (Hint: it's not Stanford.)

But the bigger point is that as long as both squads face the same rules and know about them in advance, it's a waste of breath to complain. Stop your squawking, do your job, and coach around it.

Kelly's jump from college (with bigger rosters, a wider field, and different practice regulations) to the NFL has raised many such issues. He was asked at the NFL annual meeting press conference about his penchant for being secretive about practices at Oregon. Would he continue that in Philadelphia?

"No, not in this league. You got microphones everywhere you go and cameras everywhere you go. It's a different league, different set of rules. You adapt to the league you're in."[68]

Behind his patient mantra of "just tell me the rules" is a sense that other coaches are not as adaptable, and while they complain and moan, he'll grab the advantage of being better adjusted to reality.

Chapter 25
Don't Overcoach It. Let 'Em Go Play

It would be easy to get the impression that Chip Kelly is some kind of control freak, with his intense practices, focus on players' nutrition and sleep, and his sixteen-hour work days.

Not at all. His teams are remarkably loose, and he gives both his players and his assistant coaches unusual leeway to do their jobs.

This is another paradox that resolves itself in practice. It is precisely all that preparation that allows Chip and his players to relax and have fun during the game. That's what gives you quiet, cheerful confidence.

Comedian Bob Saget, who starred in the TV show *Full House*, follows the same approach. He is one of the few comics who really enjoys and embraces the chaos of a live comedy show, not "working the crowd" in a planned way ("What do you do for a living, sir?") but truly diving into the moment and following where it leads.

In order to get to that point, though, he works very hard in advance to nail down every detail of the show that he can control. I work as a stand-up comedian and performed with him at Helium Comedy Club in Portland for a week. As the MC, I arrived an hour before the first show of the week to check up on everything.

To my surprise, when I showed up, Saget had already been there for an hour, testing lighting and sound cues with the technician, looking at sight lines, walking into the club and seeing how everything looked from the audience's perspective. That's unheard of.

His attitude was, "I want to control everything I can control, ahead of time, so I can relax and have fun during the show."

That's Chip Kelly's approach, too. And it starts with his own experience when he was an assistant.

> "I never wanted to be micromanaged when I was a coordinator. I think it's a recipe for disaster."[69]

In particular, Chip thinks that you need to do your instruction in advance; hence his long workdays. By the time you get to game day, it's too late to instruct your coaches. At that point, the head coach just needs to let go.

> "I think you spend all week long understanding the game plan and meeting with those guys and knowing what they're doing, giving your feedback during the week, but on game day I just think that's a recipe for disaster."[70]

This attitude applies to his players, even more so. Kelly and his assistant coaches think all the time so that the players don't have to. Telling them what to do during the game will just get them thinking again and ruin all the lightning-quick reactions they developed in practice.

In 2012-13, Kelly got an extreme test of this principle. Following his commitment to open competition, he had named as his starting quarterback a kid named Marcus Mariota—an eighteen-year-old redshirt freshman who had only played regularly in one of the previous four years. (He "redshirted"—saved a year of football eligibility by only practicing and attending classes—during his first year in college and was the backup his sophomore and junior years in high school.)

Why did Chip choose Mariota? Because he outplayed everyone else in the preseason, kept improving, and simply earned it. Still, a coach wouldn't need to be a control freak to worry how this kid would handle the pressure of leading the nation's fifth-ranked team into hostile stadiums on national television.

Kelly let him play, and the results were spectacular. The rookie played within himself, showed little if any duress under pressure, handed the ball off often and—when the defense gave him an opening—broke off forty- and fifty-yard quarterback draws at sprinter speed.

In the game against California on November 10, the Bears stacked the box to stop Oregon's vaunted run game, and that strategy worked. So Mariota did exactly what Chip Kelly preaches—he took what the defense gave him.

In this case, that meant the passing game. I'll be more specific. The kid threw for 377 yards and six touchdowns, tying the Oregon TD record. Oregon won by forty-two points. After the game, a reporter asked Kelly if he thought Mariota should run more. (You see why the coach gets exasperated with these guys?) Kelly said:

> "So, he's a real sharp kid, he's a real quick learner, so the more experience he gets, the better he's gonna be. But, we haven't said anything about you know, run here. I think when you're trying to tell him to do something [like that], you're screwing him up. I think in ten games so far, he's made some pretty good decisions …"[71]

Kelly not only avoids giving players advice on game day, he'll avoid it during the week if it's not necessary. Chip studies at the feet of football itself, learning from every second of actual play, and when he gets a player who does the same—like Mariota—he has the grace to shut up and get out of the way of the learning that is already going on.

MOTIVATION

CHAPTER 26
EVERY GAME IS THE SUPER BOWL

Chip Kelly hates rivalry hype. No game should be more important than any other, as long as they all count the same in the standings. One of his most frequently repeated mantras is "Every game is the Super Bowl." You shouldn't be leaving effort on the table or saving it up for some future bowl game—because you'll never get to that level if you do.

> "If the crosstown rival is game six on your schedule, and you circle it in red, you have told your team the first five games do not count."[72]

Reporters have a lot of trouble grasping this concept. Before the "Civil War" game against Oregon State in 2011, one reporter even quoted Kelly's motto about every game being the Super Bowl and then asked if this rivalry game meant even more.

> "More important than the Super Bowl? I don't think so. It's a Super Bowl. Every game is the Super Bowl for us. So I don't know how we can get bigger than that. So when people say we diminish it, we're not diminishing it. It's the biggest game we're ever going to play. [The rivalry aspect] doesn't change anything for us."[73]

He also realizes that rivalries mean the most to older fans with long memories, not the young men actually playing the game. Oregon fans are bitterest not about natural rival Oregon State—located just forty-five miles down the Willamette Valley, in Corvallis—but about the University of Washington, whose dominance and perceived arrogance in the 1980s and 1990s still burn in the hearts of Ducks.

Asked how his players felt about this decades-old resentment, Kelly quipped:

> "At seven and eight [years old,] they were [watching] SpongeBob SquarePants. They weren't worried about Joey Harrington."[74]

At the same time, under Chip the Ducks were 8-0 against their two main rivals—Oregon State and Washington—and won those games decisively. Perhaps because the coach downplayed these rivalries.

This is just as true now that he's coaching a team that can actually get to the Super Bowl—if they don't think ahead too much. And his players are getting the message, including Michael Vick.

> "Coach Kelly told us as a team, 'Don't talk about winning the Super Bowl, just put in the hard work to get there. You talk about [it] if you get there.' So I don't think about winning the Super Bowl anymore. I just think about working hard as I can and whatever's in the future is going to come."[75]

Now that Kelly is coaching in the NFL, the Super Bowl is not just a figure of speech. It's a real possibility. If Chip does take the Eagles to the big show, he'll be ready. After all, he will then be able to say "Hey, guys, no big deal. It's just another Super Bowl."

CHAPTER 27
IT'S NOT A SIN TO GET KNOCKED DOWN. IT'S A SIN TO STAY DOWN.

Chip Kelly's first game as head coach could not have been more disastrous. Despite all his hard work and clever strategies, the Ducks lost to Boise State 19-8, and Kelly's famous offense did not rack up a single first down in the entire opening half.

The best player on his team—star running back LeGarrette Blount—got frustrated enough to punch an opponent who taunted him after the game and had to be restrained from going after fans.

So there he was, a brand-new coach whose strongest suit—offense—was stuffed by Boise State, of all teams. And faced with a tough decision to make about his best player.

Chip knuckled down and did the right thing—suspending Blount for the season. The he dusted himself off and moved forward. The Ducks lost only two more games that year, to Stanford and—in the Rose Bowl—Ohio State. Both teams were ranked seventh in the nation when they defeated Oregon.

That 10-3 record was still the worst of Kelly's coaching career, but it shows his resilience in the face of challenges that would cause many new coaches to crumble. Instead his team finished the year ranked number eleven in the nation.

That resiliency was a hallmark of the Chip Kelly Ducks. It led them to tough it out through an incredible run of injuries in November of 2012, as they got ready for their toughest opponent—Stanford. Stanford is the only team that defeated Kelly twice, but they needed a field goal in overtime—and two misses by Oregon's kicker—to give the Ducks their only loss of the season.

There are many elements of Chip's program that contribute to this toughness. One is that his teams' conditioning and relentless attack wear down opponents. The Ducks dramatically outscored opponents in the fourth quarter, which gives his players confidence that the best is always ahead.

Another aspect has been smart halftime adjustments by the coaching staff, not just Kelly but also his key assistants, notably Oregon's defensive coordinator Nick Aliotti.

But much of it is mental and relates to the same even-keel emotional state that Kelly encourages—where every game is the Super Bowl, no rival is more important, no one is thinking ahead to glory. The focus is always to perform the next play as well as possible. That is the only thing that matters. And that attitude keeps you in the game, whatever the scoreboard says.

It's particularly important to avoid emotional letdowns after setbacks. When the Ducks lost a nail-biter to USC in 2011, Kelly told reporters:

> "I saw the 'Feel Sorry For Yourself' train leaving
> the parking lot, and none of our players were on it.
> So that was a good sign."[76]

This is every bit as true during a game. When someone gets injured, the Ducks feel bad, but the attitude is "next man in." One reason Kelly goes for it on fourth down and short yardage is that he has confidence in his defense to handle a tough situation, whether it's a turnover on downs, a fumble, or an interception.

> "Just because you turned it over doesn't mean the
> other team is allowed to score."[77]

And so often under Kelly's leadership, the defense has rewarded his trust. In the 2011 PAC-12 Championship Game against UCLA, the Ducks offense had yielded two turnovers and a punt by the end of the first quarter—yet the Duck defense was stiff and Oregon led 21-7.[78]

As a result, Oregon fans have gotten used to comebacks. In 2010, Stanford—their toughest opponent in the Chip years—

ran up a quick 21-3 first quarter lead against the Ducks. Oregon stayed steady and eventually crushed the Cardinal, 52-31.

Even when they lose, they fight until the end and keep it close. In the 2011 National Championship Game, the Ducks trailed a very tough Auburn team most of the game, then tied it with 2:33 left in the fourth quarter on a touchdown and clutch two-point conversion. They lost in overtime after a fluke play and a field goal but never stopped fighting.

This year, in the 2013-14 NFL season, Chip Kelly lost five of his first eight games. He only lost seven games in four years before coming to Philadelphia, but he will almost certainly lose that many or more in just this season. He knew that coming into this year, but that doesn't make it any easier to lose.

The low point of the early season was in games seven and eight, against the Dallas Cowboys and New York Giants. Starting quarterback Mike Vick was injured, so Nick Foles started against Dallas. He had the worst game of his career, missing at least eight open receivers before getting knocked out of the game with a concussion.

Against the Giants, Vick tried to come back before fully healing his hamstring and was ineffective for a half before he was reinjured. Both games were finished by third-string quarterback rookie Matt Barkley, who moved the team but turned the ball over time after time on interceptions and fumbles.

Chip Kelly's famous offense ground to a halt. Philadelphia lost to its bitter rival Dallas 17-3, and to New York (which was 1-6 at that point) by a score of 15-7. And those seven points against the Giants came from a fumble recovered and run back by the defense! The Eagles' offense, which had been averaging nearly twenty-eight points a game and setting team records, managed only three points in two entire games. Philadelphia fell to 3-5.

Through all of this, Chip Kelly maintained an even temperament. He stuck to his guns, didn't blame players for team problems, and pointed out (quite correctly) that his defense was improving rapidly. The team followed his lead and kept their heads up.

In the next game, on the road at Oakland, the Eagles won 49-20 as Nick Foles came back from his concussion to throw seven touchdowns with no interceptions and a perfect 158.3 quarterback rating. How good was that performance? Foles tied the record for touchdown passes in a game and was immediately put into the Football Hall of Fame in Canton, Ohio alongside such legends as Y.A. Tittle, Peyton Manning, Joe Kapp, and George Blanda.

The next week they beat division leader Green Bay 17-13 to move into a tie for first place in the NFC East (which was admittedly a weak conference). That was the Eagles' fifth win of the season, more than they had in all of 2012.

We know from his experience at Oregon that Chip Kelly is a good winner. As we near the end of his first year in the NFL, it looks like he'll be a pretty good loser, too.[79]

CHAPTER 28
PRESSURE IS WHAT YOU FEEL WHEN YOU DON'T KNOW WHAT YOU'RE DOING

In 2011, Chip Kelly was asked about his young squad and how he would describe their collective personality. He used two words not often seen together:

> "I think they're fearless, first and foremost. They're fun. It's a real fun group to be around. ... The two words that come to mind are fearless and fun."[80]

This was not an accident. It's precisely as the coach planned—the mental reward for all the hard work of practice. Chip described his approach after his first day of organized team activities (OTAs) with the Eagles:

> "... the game is about making quick decisions. It's a game of sixty to seventy to eighty four-second plays. So once the ball is snapped, it happens at that tempo. ... The mission is to be prepared to play a four-second play. You need to have that kind of [snapping fingers] to get that done, so I think that's why we're practicing like that."[81]

Preparation is not just learning plays but getting used to the pace and decision making of game situations. Once you've mastered all of that, you become fearless. You get "in the zone."

Nervousness and pressure are all in the mind. The goal of Kelly's practice regimen is to move beyond thinking and play instinctively. Once you stop thinking, the pressure goes away.

CHAPTER 29
PLAY WITH EMOTION, DON'T
<u>LET EMOTION PLAY WITH YOU</u>

Steadiness of emotions is a theme that runs throughout Chip Kelly's programs. He summed it up succinctly at the start of the 2011 season:

> "We respect every opponent we play. We fear none."[82]

Kelly learned the importance of this in his first game, the disastrous loss at Boise State where LeGarrette Blount lost his cool, punched an opponent, and rushed the taunting fans in the stands. Sean Devine, the offensive line coach at Boston College, was a colleague of Kelly's from New Hampshire and talked him through that low point. He puts it this way:

> "I think his point [after the Boise State game] was a valid one, that you can't be defined by the actions of one individual and one game. You can't let your emotions control you. Chip said that to our kids [in New Hampshire] all the time."[83]

Kelly's teams gradually adopted his Zen attitude, and emotional problems dwindled as the wins piled up. After leading Oregon to a stunning 47-20 victory over USC in 2009, a huge game that marked the end of the Trojans' seven-year dynasty, quarterback Jeremiah Masoli told a reporter that he and "LaMike" were cracking jokes during the game. "That's the most relaxed I've been in my career,"[84] Masoli said.

Marcus Mariota is the quintessential Chip Kelly player—large (six four), extremely fast for his position (he runs the forty-meter dash in 4.4 seconds), a quick learner, and unemotional. Kelly says:

> "I can't recall seeing him rattled. He's just a laid-back dude. He's the same all the time. And I think that's a real admirable quality to have. There's a consistency to his approach every day."[85]

The Ducks 2012 spring intrasquad game essentially decided the tight quarterback competition between Mariota—who had sat out three of the previous four years, going back to when he was fifteen—and seasoned backup quarterback Bryan Bennett.

Suddenly the young Hawaiian with just one year of experience as a starter—in high school, at that—was playing for control of a top ten football team in front of forty thousand screaming fans at Autzen Stadium. After his team won decisively, reporters asked the eighteen-year-old if he had been nervous. He said:

> "I just went out there and had fun. I had fun playing the game that I love."[86]

Kelly loves this mentality, which is simultaneously playful and professional.

> "He's got that Hawaiian island, laid back, cool breeze kind of attitude. It helps him. [But] when he puts it into gear like he did on that long run, he may be thinking like a laid-back guy, but he can run faster than a laid-back guy, I can tell you that."[87]

Part of this relaxation came from Mariota's quiet leadership, knowing that the team was behind him.

> "It was just earning the locker room's trust that I could do it. These guys around me elevated me because they knew I could do it. I just really got the ball out to those guys and they made the plays. It was a good confidence booster and I'm just looking forward to getting better."[88]

They seem like an odd couple: the fast-talking, blue collar New England ball buster and the tall, regal Samoan kid with that casual confidence that Hawaiians call "local-boy style."[89] But underneath the surface differences, they share a rock-solid and hard-earned confidence, and they recognize it in each other.

For Chip Kelly, one of the hardest parts of leaving the Ducks must have been giving up three years of coaching Marcus. Three potential years, anyway; it's unlikely Mariota will finish four years before the NFL calls him away, especially after Matt Barkley's disastrous experience returning to USC for his senior year.

Whenever he does go pro, don't be surprised if Kelly goes to great lengths to acquire him for the Eagles.

CHAPTER 30
PLAY FROM A DESIRE TO EXCEL, NOT A FEAR OF FAILURE

For all the intense practices and long hours, the people in Kelly's programs have fun. Their love of the game, the emphasis on team play and cooperation, and the unique team identity combine to create a buy-in among players that is unusual.

It remains to be seen if older, jaded professionals will be as open to embracing this unusual system, but comprehensive programs and successful results go a long way toward persuading even the cockiest pro. After all, Phil Jackson was able to get the likes of Kobe Bryant, Shaquille O'Neal, Dennis Rodman, and Michael Jordan on board with Lakota war drums and burning sage around the locker room—and ended up with eleven championships as a coach. Compared to that, a wise-ass New Englander who wants to run opponents into the ground should have no trouble at all.

Kelly does a couple of things that go a long way toward building loyalty among his players, techniques that are fully applicable to any leader in business or government. The first is that he takes the time to explain why they do unusual things. Eagles wide receiver Jason Avant told Don Banks of *Sports Illustrated*:

> "One thing I like about Chip is you can go in and ask him why am I doing this, why am I running this route instead of this route, and he'll tell you, boom, boom, boom. That makes you respect him more and it gives you a place where you can voice your opinion. Not to be disagreeable but just to let

him know you're trying to learn. He doesn't take it as a threat. ...

"Everything has a purpose. If it's not proven, we won't do it."[90]

Philadelphia's center Jason Kelce agrees.

"The way they explain things, it makes it easy to understand why you're doing this. They explain why hydrating is important, they explain why sleep is important, they explain why doing the lifts we do is important. So everything has a meaning to it, and he'll never hide the reason we're doing things."[91]

When you're trying to innovate in a very traditional sport, this open communication is crucial. And the lack of defensiveness is even more crucial. It's not about the coach being right; it's about finding out what works, and players ultimately are in the best position to say what brings them to their best level of performance.

The second thing Kelly does is to trust players with a lot of responsibility and lets the results determine his decisions, without getting into blaming, punishment, and other ego-driven negativity.

Often, when things go badly, leaders criticize underlings out of their own fear, unwilling to take personal responsibility for the failure of their program. It serves both to deflect blame and offer a little cheap emotional relief, like kicking your dog after a tough day, but it poisons the work environment.

Chip Kelly doesn't do that. After all, if someone is doing what the coach asks, how could he get mad at them, in fairness? All he asks is that people improve.

The Ducks played Louisiana State University (LSU) at the start of the 2011 season. It was their first outing since narrowly losing the national championship the previous January to another SEC team, Auburn. The game was heavily hyped and nationally televised, the first opening game matchup of top five teams on a neutral field in twenty-seven years.

A lot of attention was focused on true freshman De'Anthony Thomas, a flashy football and track star that Oregon had stolen away from USC on signing day the previous spring.

Thomas scored a touchdown in the waning seconds, but he fumbled on two consecutive plays in the third quarter. LSU scored after both turnovers, for 14 points in a game they won by thirteen, 40 to 27. ESPN's wrap-up said, "It was over when … LSU scored back-to-back TDs in the third quarter following De'Anthony Thomas fumbles."[92]

Afterward reporters practically begged Kelly to blame Thomas. Instead the coach said:

> "Our players play from a desire to excel—not a fear of failure. I'm not yanking a kid when he puts the ball on the ground. As I learned from [basketball coach] Paul Westhead a long time ago, you may stop the bleeding, but you may kill the patient and that's not going to happen here."[93]

Once again, Kelly de-emphasized personalities and emotion and refocused on execution. He wasn't happy about the fumbles, but the solution was not to yell at the freshman or bench him. The solution was to teach him how to protect the ball. De'Anthony Thomas went on to have an outstanding season as the Ducks won the Rose Bowl.

CHIP

CHAPTER 31
BIG BALLS CHIP

During the 2012 off-season, Kelly took a little break from his long work days and flew to Spain—where he ran with the bulls down the streets of Pamplona. Afterward he told the press:

> "If someone says they did it and they weren't scared, then they're lying."[94]

But if Chip feels fear like everyone else, he seems to feel it less often.

Kelly's coaching is marked by aggressive plays, two-point conversions, and fourth down runs. Against ninth-ranked Stanford in 2010, down 21-3 early, he called an onside kick after Oregon scored a touchdown—early in the *second quarter*.[95] This stunning maneuver swung the momentum, sparking Oregon's comeback, and the Ducks won 52-31.

These are not wild gambles, however. In the Stanford game, special teams coach Tom Osborne had observed a flaw in Stanford's discipline while studying game film. Some of their front four on kick returns were running backward too early, before they saw the kick go deep, and Oregon had practiced an onside kick all week.

The fourth down tries and two-point conversions also are statistically smart.[96] But it still takes guts to call them, and Chip's style is marked in general by his aggressive confidence—a confidence born from hard work, practice, and careful preparation.

On October 15, 2011, ESPN was getting ready to interview Kelly for their GameDay broadcast, and they couldn't understand what the large crowd of Duck fans was chanting as they connected his microphone. The chant turned out to be "Big Balls Chip," a common nickname in Oregon that has spawned a number of amusing T-shirts.

If you don't believe that this is a common nickname, just Google "Chip Kelly." In the info box that appears on the right of the screen, look and see what it says under "Nicknames."

Chip Kelly

Football coach

Charles "Chip" Kelly is an American football coach. He is currently the head coach of the Philadelphia Eagles and the former head coach at the University of Oregon. Wikipedia

Born: November 25, 1963 (age 50), Dover, NH

Team: Philadelphia Eagles

Past teams coached: Oregon Ducks football (Head coach, 2009–2012)

Education: University of New Hampshire, Manchester Central High School

Nicknames: Big Balls Chip, Chip

Parents: Paul Kelly, Jean Kelly

CHAPTER 32
SOMETIMES I CAN BE SARCASTIC.
I DON'T KNOW IF PEOPLE REALIZE THAT.

In 2007, some fans in Eugene, Oregon were in line to buy basketball tickets and killing time by tossing a football around. A husky stranger interrupted to give them some unsolicited advice:

> "Let me show you how to throw a football. You gotta flick it like a booger."[97]

The stranger was Oregon's new offensive coordinator (and former high school quarterback) Chip Kelly. He's a very funny guy, a classic New England deadpan ball-buster.

He also doesn't see the need to give anyone respect that they haven't earned. And he is surrounded by very talented people who have been working their asses off for most of their lives, so his standards for earning respect are very high.

This has led to an often-contentious relationship with the press, whose members are not used to being challenged and rarely have the history of military service or major football accomplishment (either as a player or coach) that most impresses Chip.

When Kelly was at the University of Oregon, there was also a bit of a West Coast/East Coast culture clash, something that won't be a problem in Philadelphia (where fans are known to throw batteries and boo Santa Claus). But Oregon is definitely laid back, if a bit more solid than California.

I experienced Chip's culture clash in the opposite direction, as an Oregon kid who went to college in Boston. Out of the blue—in a Store 24, for example—total strangers kept giving me crap, and I thought "Oh my God, every single person is an asshole here!"

Of course, four years later when I returned to Portland, *I* was the asshole, busting chops on people I just met and offending baffled strangers. I had to become a stand-up comedian just to explain myself.

Still, it's Chip Kelly's jousting with the press that we hear about the most because even when reporters are the butt of the joke, they can't ignore the fact that Kelly gives some of the best interviews in sports. For full effect, you need to know that he talks very fast and right off the top of his head. Here are some examples.

At the press conference after the 2013 NFL annual meeting, a reporter asked whether Kelly's Eagles would use the read option play he relied on at Oregon.

> "It depends on who your QB is. If you were my
> QB, (probably not). You have to adapt."[98]

Another asked him what had been the most difficult thing to deal with in Philadelphia. Kelly replied, "The Schuylkill [Expressway]."[99]

At the press conference on the first day of organized team activities—a non-contact set of drills—he was asked to rate how well his team played.

> "Our defense was going against barrels, and our
> offense was going against air. But our offense
> killed it against air, so if we could play air we'd be
> really good ..."[100]

Kelly makes it very clear that he does not give out information about the current injury status of his players. This has been his consistent policy for many years, as reporters know.

In one of Kelly's first moves as coach, the Eagles signed free agent Kenny Phillips, a talented but wounded veteran coming back from microfracture surgery in his left knee in 2009 and an MCL problem in his right knee in 2012. After Phillips sat out one of the Eagles' early practices, some reporter asked the coach, "Does (Kenny Phillips) have an injury?" Kelly's answer:

"Yeah, he's had an injury for a couple of years now."[101]

Many of Chip's best quips have involved bringing reporters who get too clever in their thinking back down to earth. When one reporter asked what he had learned from studying USC's epic run of seven straight PAC-10 championships (from 2002-2008), Kelly answered "Yeah. Get good players." The Trojans were (and are) a recruiting giant of almost SEC proportions, clearly dominant in the PAC-12.

Some of these busts are so deadpan that people might even miss them. After a rare loss, one reporter asked how much he planned to change his strategy as a result.

"Thirteen percent. Exactly."[102]

Kelly doesn't like long-winded speeches or stuffiness in any form, either. Before the 2011 National Championship Game, after endless interviews and speculation, there was this exchange:

> "MODERATOR: We will take an opening statement from Coach Kelly.
>
> KELLY: From me? Wow. Haven't heard enough? Game is tomorrow night. Let's go play. Questions?"[103]

On a similar note, after Oregon beat UCLA for the 2011 PAC-12 championship, the press conference moderator asked if there were any opening statements. Kelly quipped:

> "Opening statements? Is this a debate? LaMichael: Thermonuclear war. Are you for it or against it?"[104]

He also doesn't like stupid questions. One reporter at spring training in Oregon noted that then-new recruit Colt Lyerla had started workouts at tight end. He asked, does that mean you want him to play tight end? Chip said:

> "We were actually going to look at him at D-lineman, but we couldn't get the right jersey on him. No, we are going to look at him at tight end.

That is why we put him at tight end."[105]

It's not just that Kelly thinks he's smarter and funnier than everybody else (though I'm not saying that he doesn't or that he isn't). This is part of the New Hampshire culture he grew up in, and it's a way for him to stay grounded, as his oldest friends will tell you. Kevin Mills, an assistant coach at Portsmouth High School and one of Kelly's best friends, said this:

> "Some people, you put a couple dollars in their pocket, and they sort of drift away, go Hollywood. He hasn't done that at all. Whenever I go to a New Hampshire game, he's texting me, asking me what's going on."[106]

Sean Devine, the offensive line coach at Boston College, confirms this:

> "He likes to bust (chops). He's quick-witted with a great sense of humor. (But) he's a good guy. My first couple years, when I was a young coach and I was making peanuts, he took great care of me. Many times we'd hang out in Portsmouth, and he'd take care of things."[107]

Mills again:

> "Loves to laugh. He's the king of trying to bust peoples' chops."[108]

There's a serious business behind the chop-busting. It's a way to stay grounded, to keep your ego in check, to keep the focus on results and earned trust. Kelly has paid to fly half a dozen old friends from New Hampshire in for a few games every year, even when he was across the country in Oregon. The loyalty of someone you can trust to give you crap is valuable. Mike Zamarchi, a high school coach and old friend of Kelly's, said:

> "I think he likes us coming out. It loosens him up a little bit. He can be who he is, who he's always been. Most people just know him since he became

the head coach at Oregon."[109]

A reporter once asked Kelly why he is so contentious with the media, while he famously bonds with his players:

> "I'm different with our players because I trust our players and I'm with them every day, and I understand what they're all about. I'm like that with everybody. It ain't going to be Kumbaya and hug you the first time I meet you. But if I see you every day and understand what you're about every day and that you share the same vision that I have, then I'll die for you."[110]

One of the many contentious issues that the press asked Kelly about was how long he would stay at Oregon and whether he planned to go to the NFL. Did it make it hard to recruit for the Ducks, one reporter asked, after he started talking to teams like Tampa Bay about coaching positions? Chip's answer was classic:

> "I'd have a hard time saying, 'Hey, please come to my program cause we're really mediocre and I'll never get offered a job anywhere else.'"[111]

Reporters kept grilling him, and Kelly threw it right back. Eugene, Oregon is a town of only 150,000 people, and the newspaper is pretty small. Reporter Adam Jude from the *Eugene Register-Guard* asked the coach if he was being honest with recruits that he might not be there for their entire playing career. Kelly said absolutely and came right back at the reporter:

> "I don't think anybody can say where they're going to be four years from now. Can you tell me that you're going to be at the *Register-Guard* for four years? I wanna get you on record, too. Are we locking you in?"[112]

That reporter, Adam Jude, left his paper for the larger and better-paying *Oregonian* six months later, half a year before Kelly took the job in Philadelphia.

CHAPTER 33
THE TAO OF CHIP KELLY

When I say "The Tao of Chip Kelly," I'm not speaking in the generic sense, meaning just a way of doing something.

I'm specifically talking about Tao as in the ancient Chinese philosophy of Taoism. Kelly has never spoken publicly about the Tao (also known as "the Way"), and he may never have read about or even heard of it. His tastes seem to run more to motivational business books, such as *Grow the Bamboo* by ex-Duck Greg Bell and *Good to Great* by Jim Collins.[113] But his football program is a near-perfect implementation of secular Taoist principles.

Taoism is not cute and cuddly, despite the success of Benjamin Hoff's book, *The Tao of Pooh*. The two original books of Taoism, the *Chuang Tzu* and the *Tao Te Ching*, celebrate butchers, competitive archers, and men that train fighting roosters, all of whom succeed by following the Way.

These books were written during China's Warring States Period (around 500 to 300 B.C.E.) as advice for rulers of small kingdoms on how to prevail against their enemies—a pretty good parallel for top-level football coaches.

Religious forms of Taoism with multiple gods, parallels to Buddhism, and appeals to a "celestial bureaucracy" developed hundreds of years later, starting around 142 C.E.,[114] but in its earliest forms, we know only of the spare and paradoxical philosophy best expressed in these two books.

Much of Taoism revolves around the limits and dangers of thinking, words, labels, and categories. These things are hallmarks of civilization, of course, but Taoists also see how they limit understanding and peak performance. When we say someone is "in their head," we all know that they are thinking too much and underperforming as a result.

Practical Taoism involves techniques to move beyond thinking into intuitive, finely honed instinct. Think martial artists, not philosophers. A Taoist doesn't discuss his theory or ideology; he talks about his "practice." Not "what do you think about this?" but "what do you do to improve yourself?"

Above all, Taoism is practical and reality-based; it's a Way of doing things, whatever those things might be. Kelly's de facto Taoism involves four key aspects of the game: understanding, strategy, execution (based on practice), and attitude.

1. UNDERSTANDING

The Way of Taoism starts with direct perception—not mediated through words and statistics—and intuitive insights developed through long experience and focused, humble observation. *Chuang Tzu* in particular celebrates modest workmen who master the Tao by practicing their physical craft for years, whether it's cutting up oxen, training roosters to fight, or crafting wooden bell stands.

Football is Chip Kelly's physical craft, one he has pursued since his teenage years as a player. He is an avid student of football, always eager to learn from competing coaches or share his knowledge. While he was still an assistant at New Hampshire, he would travel on his own dime during the off-season to confer with other spread offense coaches, whether they worked in high schools, major college programs, or the pros.

One such visit so impressed the coach at Oregon, Mike Bellotti, that he later recruited Kelly as his offensive coordinator and heir. More recently, Bill Belichick (New England's legendary coach) called Kelly in for pointers on the no-huddle offense the Patriots were refining.

Kelly played football at the University of New Hampshire (QB and defensive back) and methodically worked his way up the coaching ranks over seventeen years, starting as a low-level assistant at Columbia before he went to Oregon. His knowledge is deep and intuitive, rooted in many years of experience. No surprise, then, that he can get frustrated at sportswriters, who truck in words, theories, and diagrams.

Direct experience also drives his open competitions for playing time and starting positions. Talent, reputation, size, and past glory do not sway Kelly. With his unusual style of play that relies heavily on split-second decisions, actual performance (in training camp, practice, and games) is the fairest and most reliable way to decide who gets minutes and reps. And the large number of reps in practice gives Kelly's staff plenty of pre-game data, not based on coaches' projections but on who really works best with the team.

Watching the players in person is the best way to evaluate them, and video is a close second. Seeing a team in action gives a much deeper understanding than game statistics or the words of someone who scouted a player. You are observing a number of things that you might not even be conscious of, and analyzing the details disrupts that direct, unmediated perception. Sometimes breaking something down just leaves you with broken pieces instead of the whole.

Kelly has the courage to go where the results lead him, even if they are unexpected. At Oregon, Chip's open competitions led him to choose redshirt freshman Marcus Mariota over the more seasoned Bryan Bennett, just as he had earlier picked Darron Thomas over veteran Nate Costa.

Kelly is a gardener who throws out a bunch of seeds, waiting to see which grow best in the soil he's tilled. Rather than prejudging the best seed stock, he simply picks the ones that thrive. The result is a series of unheralded recruits, like Thomas, Mariota, and Dennis Dixon, who routinely surprise with their success because they fit the team and the program organically. The quarterback becomes the star, and the coach fades into the background. As Chuang Tzu wrote, "When the shoe fits, the foot is forgotten."

2. STRATEGY

Despite what you might have read, the Oregon Ducks do not pass much, their quarterback doesn't run that often, and they don't use the pistol formation. Kelly's offense relies on a sort of artful simplicity that goes to the heart of Taoist philosophy.

His spread formation is designed to give his team access to every inch of the field and force the defense to reveal its strategy. The skill players then have multiple options to punish that defensive strategy, and the speed and downfield blocking by receivers can turn small openings into big gains.

The very first page of the *Tao Te Ching* discusses the dangers of naming things, labeling, and categorizing. These are very powerful tools for communicating and for conceptualizing the world, but if we mistake the label for the thing it describes, we understand only the label and not the thing itself.

Kelly has realized that fixed plays and positions in football have the same effect. While easier to explain to players and reporters, rigid positions and plays artificially limit what your eleven players can do. If you recruit specific physical types to fit those positions and plays, you limit yourself even more. In conventional football, one hybrid position like the H-back is considered a major innovation. Kelly aims for a deeper simplicity, blurring distinctions between all of his backs—"players, not positions" as Tommy Lawlor of Igglesblitz.com puts it.[115] Under Kelly's system, for example, the Ducks' De'Anthony Thomas was listed as a running back, but he played in the slot, got most of his yardage on passes, and played on special teams as both returner and gunner.

Traditional football plays are fixed and rigid, like the nineteenth century land wars that football was modeled after. If the defense is prepared and forces the offense to abandon its strategy after the ball is snapped, we call the result "a broken play," and any successful improvisation by the guy with the ball is seen as a minor miracle. Even a touchdown off of a "broken play" is considered an anomaly, more luck than success.

Chip's plays, in contrast, are designed to react flexibly to several different defensive responses and take whatever the offense is given. The key is not tipping your hand until you see that defensive response. Once you see it, then you make your choice as to what your offense is going to do and be for that one play.

Similarly, Taoists like to talk of the "uncarved block," a piece of wood with the potential to become anything—milled lumber, an elegant sculpture, split firewood, or sawdust. As soon as you define it, by making something out of it, you destroy all those other possibilities. Kelly's offense is an uncarved block, built around a few flexible formations. With running backs who catch passes, tight ends (and quarterbacks) who run, receivers who block, and read-option plays that don't reveal the choice until the middle of the play, Kelly preserves all of his team's choices as late as possible. That type of flexibility is hard to coach against.

For example, the read-option play is designed to let the quarterback identify where the defense is positioning its floating players and—to paraphrase baseball wag Willie Keeler—"run where they ain't." Every coach would love to know what his opponent plans to do and then be able to call a play to counter that. Kelly has figured out how to let his quarterback do this, in real time, as long as the coach gives up some of his control.

He sacrifices his own ego by giving his players more choices. This allows the offense to wait until the very last millisecond to make a decision. Unless the defense is very disciplined and fast, and has a like-minded coach, they will have to make their move first, based on their coach's call, and the offense will be able to respond to that choice. But how will the opposing coach know what to do? You can't plan for a play that hasn't been defined yet.

Kelly spelled his basic theories out in detail in a series of lectures he gave for Nike as part of their "Coach of the Year" workshops. Basically, if the defense plays two safeties, you run. If they pull both up to stop the run, you pass. If they play one safety, the quarterback can "block" a defender by "reading" him—noting his position—and steering the play in the other direction, thus regaining the advantage.

If it sounds simple, it is. Kelly has the confidence to not be clever, if not-clever works. Unlike, say, a Steve Spurrier, Chip has no need to show off his intricate play-calling.

In the 2013 Fiesta Bowl, Oregon was leading Kansas State

just 15-10 right before the half. They ran five plays in a key scoring drive, and three were identical—the "PA-Vert."[116] The first two PA-Verts were both big gains to six foot six tight end Colt Lyerla over the middle. (Hey, if they don't adjust, just keep pounding it home.) On the third repetition, three Kansas State backs surrounded Lyerla, including the man who had been marking Kenjon Barner as he came out of the backfield. Barner, wide open, caught a pass in the flat and ran twenty-four yards for the touchdown. The entire drive covered seventy-seven yards in forty-six seconds. Kelly had begun each play with the same block of wood; on the last, the players carved out seven points.

At the same time, Kelly remains unpredictable, allowing many possibilities for the final manifestation of the wood block. Charles Fischer, the founder of FishDuck.com, notes that Kelly's game plans contain fewer plays than most—forty-five or so, against a more typical eighty—but he usually includes a surprise, especially in big games. In the 2013 Fiesta Bowl, for example, Kelly pulled out a play used only once that season, another not used since the 2011 game against LSU and a formation not seen since 2009. "He keeps changing the tumblers on the locks," Fischer notes, "more than any other coach I've seen."[117]

Typically these surprises are not flashy or trick plays. Many viewers and even reporters may not notice, but opponents are unlikely to have prepared against them. They keep the defense off guard, and—given Oregon's speed and downfield blocking—any sizable hole can result in fifty yards or seven points.

At Philadelphia, Kelly already is bringing in more flexibility and extending the concepts even further. The Eagles' wide receivers will, for the first time, have option routes, which they can change on the fly based on how the defense covers them. And where the Ducks used a no-huddle offense with a single play called from the sidelines via a giant four-part sign, Kelly's Eagles will have a new, even wilder system. Position coaches will use hand signals to call different plays for different groups of players. Obviously these won't be traditional football plays but more specific strategies; block here, run there, expect this.

Lao Tzu wrote that rulers should, "Govern a great nation

as you would cook a small fish; do not overdo it." Like Lao Tzu's sage king, Kelly understands that a light touch delivers the best leadership.

3. EXECUTION

> "If your players have not run that [game-deciding play] over a thousand times in practice, you will not have a chance to be successful. ... My old high school coach told me a long time ago that 'If your head is moving, your feet are not.' That means if you are thinking about what to do, you are not doing it as fast." —Chip Kelly[118]

> "When I first began to cut up oxen, I saw nothing but oxen. After three years of practicing, I no longer saw the ox as a whole. I now work with my spirit, not with my eyes. My senses stop functioning and my spirit takes over. I follow the natural grain, letting the knife find its way through the many hidden openings, taking advantage of what is there ..." – Chuang Tzu, 300 B.C.E.[119]

A coach's plays and schemes, however clever, don't win games. Execution by his players wins games. Chip Kelly has a detailed method for improving his players' performance at game time, and—just as with the ancient butcher of oxen—it revolves around practice.

It's easy to see what Kelly considers the heart of his program. He has published a total of three articles on coaching, based on his talks at the Nike Coach of the Year clinics. The last two are "Efficient Use of Practice Time" and "Practice Organization: The Key to Success."

As we saw in Chapter 18—and as Kelly discussed in the former article—he emphasizes learning by doing. The only truly reliable memory is muscle memory.

Chip Kelly's practices are unlike any other coach's. Reporters fixate on the intense speed of practice and blaring up-tempo music, but the most striking thing is the minimal amount of talking. To Kelly, practice is for one thing: repetitions. Learning by doing. Teaching and talking takes place in classrooms and video sessions beforehand, wherever possible. Stopping to talk during practice is a wasted opportunity and pulls you away from the rhythm of actual games.

As much as possible, every aspect of practice emulates the game environment. If you can't stop a play and instruct your player in a game, don't do that in practice. Kelly's assistants only correct players if they are substituted out of the scrimmage. The loud music is designed in part to simulate game conditions, specifically players' inability to communicate without shouting or hand signals, but also the excitement of the event. It's an exercise in focus despite distractions.

Brian Smith of the website Grantland put it this way:

> "Without time wasted huddling, players get many more practice repetitions, leading to increased efficiency on Saturdays. As Sam Snead once said, 'practice is putting brains in your muscles,' and Oregon's up-tempo practices are all about making Kelly's system second nature."[120]

The only way to get players ready to play is to play. At game speed, you literally don't have time to think. To read your opponents and adjust in real time, you must use your well-honed instinct, and the only way to develop that is by running plays, over and over and over. Kelly wants the ball out of the quarterback's hands in 1.5 seconds on each play (unless the QB runs). That leaves no time for thinking, words, or even concepts. You have to be in the zone.

Kelly's practices start fast and keep accelerating. His Ducks typically ran 135 plays in each practice and sometimes more than 150. Several players have said that games seem slow in comparison. The Ducks ran no wind sprints; the entire practice was a wind sprint in the form of reps.

The extra plays—and Kelly's aggressive substitution patterns—also let the coach give a lot of reps to players further down the depth chart. At Oregon, Kelly played nine different quarterbacks in his first three years and didn't miss a beat because his replacements were as practiced as his starters. When he had to suspend starting quarterback Jeremiah Masoli after a burglary conviction, unheralded backup Darron Thomas—who had only played in five games before that season—took the Ducks to the National Championship Game.

Kelly also has a sophisticated understanding of football as a dynamic sport. Players are young and careers are short. Each athlete changes from game to game and practice rep to practice rep as they grow, age, gain experience, and suffer injuries. The first game of a season has a different rhythm than the second to last; pre-contract drills have a specific nature, and there's no point in treating them the same as a full scrimmage. During the season, the week before a game has its own pulse unconnected to the normal calendar. Even players' sleep cycles must be accepted and worked with.

Everything has its own dynamic rhythm, which Taoists call tzu-jan—things unfolding according to their own nature. A wise leader is able to perceive—to feel—them all interacting with each other and works to synchronize them like a symphony orchestra. This is the deep and powerful sense of timing that gives a Taoist sage his or her power, and Chip Kelly clearly has mastered it for his football teams.

Kelly's teams slice through defenses and find the hidden openings just like the master butcher slicing his ox, but that elegance is not derived from magic. It comes from practice.

4. ATTITUDE

Every coach strives to focus and motivate their players and manage their emotions—especially in college, where most students are suddenly the big stars on campus, not fully matured, and usually living away from home for the first time.

Chip Kelly's efforts, however, are based on concepts more common in Eastern philosophy books than Super Bowl highlight films: be present in the moment; minimize ego; ignore rewards, criticism, and comparisons with others; stay dispassionate and disciplined through hard work.

This philosophy manifests in ways that counter football tradition. With all due respect to Knute Rockne, Kelly is not one for stirring half-time speeches. He told a reporter in 2010,

> "There's no time for some rousing speech. It's businesslike. We play a full 60 minutes."[121]

Like a Taoist sage, Kelly discourages comparisons with other in favor of self-discipline and cultivation. Before the 2011 season, when asked about the Ducks' number three preseason ranking, he replied:

> "We have the same mentality all the time. We have a vision for what this football program is supposed to be about, and we go out and compete against that vision every Saturday. That's how we measure ourselves, and that's what we're concerned with. We're not concerned with any outside influences, whether it be praise or blame. It's all the same to us."[122]

Rather than competing and comparing, Kelly pushes his team to self-cultivation, improving their own performance, and execution. They develop mastery on their own terms and let opponents figure out what they want to do about it.

Ted Miller of ESPN summed it up nicely:

> "Oregon, steadfastly adhering to coach Chip Kelly's philosophies, only plays nameless, faceless opponents. And every week is a Super Bowl. There are no rivalries. There are no special emotions. The idea is simple. You should always be 100 percent focused on the task at hand because 75 percent means you're letting your team down and 110 percent is hyperbole."[123]

Much of American sports mythology revolves around emotion, which drives the narrative of the heroic win. Kelly's teams are more like the fighting rooster in chapter 19 of *Chuang Tzu*.[124] The king had asked Chi Hsing Tzu to train an unbeatable rooster and kept asking impatiently if it was ready yet. After ten days, the trainer says no because the rooster still picks fights. Another ten, and it still reacted at the sound of another rooster crowing. Even after thirty days, the rooster was not ready, as he ruffled his feathers and got an angry look.

Only after forty days did Chi Hsing Tzu think the rooster was ready. Why? Because he stood immobile, as if he was made of wood, even when another rooster crowed. As the trainer proudly observed, other birds will take one look at him and run away.

When you put these four elements together—understanding, strategy, execution, and attitude—Kelly has constructed a comprehensive program that encompasses the physical, mental, and even spiritual. This is precisely his goal. "What do we stand for?" he asked at the beginning of his 2011 Nike workshop. "You have to answer that in your offensive, defensive, and special team philosophies. ... People should be able to come observe you and in five minutes know what you stand for." Not concepts, not words, but results. Execution.

What do Kelly's teams stand for? The answer for Oregon was typically simple: "Fast. Play Hard. Finish." The answer for Philadelphia will certainly be different because Chip Kelly is not an ideologue. He uses his knowledge and philosophy to adapt to his situation, and his program will be dynamic, evolving, constantly adapting. But once he works it out, the answer will be succinct, and the results will be fascinating.

CHAPTER 34
THE PHILADELPHIA STORY

Coach Kelly never had to rebuild a team before he took over in Philadelphia. The Oregon Ducks have the most experienced and stable coaching staff in football; many assistants have been there twenty years or longer, and Coach Mike Bellotti had started building a spread offense two years before Kelly arrived as his offensive coordinator.

At New Hampshire, not only was Kelly never the head coach, but he held every offensive assistant coaching job before he became offensive coordinator and even played there as a an undergraduate under the same head coach.

Philadelphia was different. The Eagles were 4-12 in 2012, losing eleven of their last twelve games. The "Wide 9" defense was a disaster, and the team's talent was spotty at best. Kelly cleaned house. He hired a new coaching staff, brought in several free agents, drafted well, held open competitions for roster spots, and switched to a 3-4 "two-gap" defense.

As I write this, twelve games into his first season, the Eagles are tied with Dallas for first place in the NFC East, and already they have won three more games than in the entire previous year.

At the same time, they are not a very good team. Yet. The NFC East is the weakest division in the NFL, and the Eagles are 7-5, with losses to San Diego, Dallas, and especially the New York Giants (who were 1-6 at the time) that could have been wins.

Kelly himself has made a number of mistakes during games—in clock management, challenges not thrown, and in play-calling. The NFL is very different from college, and Kelly is a rookie, too. He needs more reps to get better, just as much as his players do.

That said, the Eagles are improving rapidly and the general outline of Kelly's program is coming into focus. Before the season began, most pundits expected the offense to be good, and the defense to be terrible. The change from a Wide 9 to a 3-4 defense is radical, and it was unclear how many players Philadelphia had that fit the new system.

The first four games were as bad as predicted. The Eagles gave up twenty-seven, thirty-three, twenty-six, and fifty-two points and lost three of those four games.

The defense toughened up faster than anyone expected, though. In games five through twelve, it gave up twenty-one or fewer points per game, the only team in the NFL that can say that. The team has still been giving up a lot of yardage, but the "bend but don't break" style typical of Kelly's Oregon Ducks—with a lot of takeaways and stout red zone defense—has emerged in his NFL team, too.

The offense has also done well, except for two games. The Eagles are setting team records. They are second in the NFL in rushing yardage after twelve games and ninth in passing.

Kelly has done an excellent job of getting the most out of his skill players. After twelve games, LeSean McCoy is second only to Adrian Peterson in rushing yards, and averages more yards per carry. DeSean Jackson is also having a career year, with over 1,000 receiving yards. Riley Cooper has emerged as a potent second option at wide receiver, filling the gap left by Jeremy Maclin's season-ending ACL tear during training camp.

The biggest issue has been at quarterback. During training camp, Michael Vick won an open competition with Nick Foles for the starting job. He passed well, despite three interceptions and some questionable decision-making, and ran brilliantly. In fact, Vick was the fifteenth best rusher in the NFL, ahead of half the league's starting RBs, when he injured his hamstring muscle.

The season's low point came in the two games after Vick's injury. Second year player Nick Foles started against the Dallas Cowboys in a showdown for first place in the division and had the worst game of his young career before being literally knocked out of the game (after holding on to the ball for a full nine seconds on a pass play).

Vick rushed back from his hamstring injury to start the next game against the woeful New York Giants but may have been too tough for his own good. He was clearly hobbled, and the Giants did not respect his ability to run. Vick was ineffective until he was reinjured and had to leave.

In both games, rookie fourth-round pick Matt Barkley came in to finish. He actually moved the team well but threw three consecutive interceptions against the Cowboys and fumbled on his first possession in the Giants game (after driving to the two yard line). The team's high-powered offense managed only three points against Dallas and none against New York (though the defense got a touchdown on a fumble recovery).

It's too soon to tell if these games were an anomaly or a sign of problems to come. Indications are good. Not many teams win in the NFL with their third-string quarterback, and Foles has been excellent since that Dallas game. For the year as a whole, he has thrown nineteen touchdown passes with no interceptions and only one fumble, and his quarterback rating of 125.2 leads the league.

The defense is much improved, especially on the very young defensive line (which has no player older than 25). The secondary, while much improved since last year, needs new blood, and the team must begin to replace its excellent but aging offensive line. But the Eagles are playing exciting football, and the rough shape of a potentially dominating team is emerging.

CHAPTER 35
GENIUS?

Chip Kelly is often called a genius. And he hates that.

> "Jonas Salk [inventor of the polio vaccine] was a genius; I coach football."[125]

I don't think this is false modesty. For one thing, the concept of the genius coach goes against every bit of his philosophy. Everything he does works to reduce the importance of the coach's schemes and play calls—because that makes his team more likely to win.

Coach Kelly also is quick to point to the football thinkers whose ideas he has used. His guru, if he has one, is the legendary coach Paul Brown. Kelly has made a point of traveling far and wide to find the best innovators in football and share ideas with them, even when he was an assistant coach paying his own way.

Chip Kelly's football prowess is not so much genius as mastery, the same mastery anyone could get—with twenty years of sixteen-hour days attentively working your ass off at the thing you love. Very few of us do that, of course. Chip did.

If Kelly has a genius, it's for clarity. Clarity of his own vision of what he wants for his teams. And clarity of communication, his amazing ability to boil complex ideas into those catchy phrases that this book is organized around.

By doing the extra work of figuring out what he wants, finding a way to make it clear to his players, and executing that vision in every aspect of his program, Chip Kelly has mastered the art of building extremely successful teams. And that is a lesson that every manager and leader can learn from.

Sources

INTRODUCTION

1   Chip Kelly, "The Zone Read Option Game," in "2009 Coach of the Year Clinics Football Manual," ed.Earl Browning (Monterey, CA: Coaches Choice), 2009, 141-7.

-   Chip Kelly, "Efficient use of practice time," in "2011 Coach of the Year Clinics Football Manual," ed. Earl Browning (Monterey, CA: Coaches Choice), 2011, 138-45.

-   Chip Kelly, "Practice Organization," in "2012 Coach of the Year Clinics Football Manual," ed. Earl Browning (Monterey, CA: Coaches Choice), 2012, 493-524.

THE PROGRAM

2   Aaron Fentress, "Ducks insider: Oregon coach Chip Kelly shrugs off NFL rumors, focuses on Fiesta Bowl," the Oregonian, December 26, 2012.

3   Laozi, Daodejing, "Chapter 64." Of course he didn't say "miles," because he was writing in the Kingdom of Chu around 300 B.C.E., before China was even solidified. The measurement they used at the time was the li, which was equivalent to about one-third of a mile. Not that the exact distance matters at all.

4   Rachel Bachman, "As Oregon Ducks 'Win the Day' over and over, motto gathers steam," the Oregonian, November 8, 2010.

5   ibid.

6   Stephen Alexander, "Chip Kelly holds court, minus assistant coaches," Portland Tribune, December 31, 2011.

7   Full Chip Kelly transcript from NFL Annual Meeting, op. cit.

8   Spike Eskin, "Chip Kelly Is The 9th Highest Paid Coach In American Sports," CBS Philly.com, May 29, 2013.

9   Mike Zhe, "Seacoast roots run deep for Oregon coach Chip Kelly," SeaCoastOnline.com, January 9, 2011.

10   Full Chip Kelly transcript from NFL Annual Meeting.

11   Charles Fischer, personal interview, May 2013.

12   Chip Kelly, "Efficient use of practice time,"

13   "Oregon Red-Zone Scoring Percentage," TeamRankings. com, captured May 2013.

14   Pete Roussel, "4-year study: Most Takeaways in College Football," CoachingSearch.com, May 13, 2013.

15   Chip Kelly, "Efficient use of practice time,"

16   Chip Kelly, "The Zone Read Option Game."

17   George Schroeder, "A Man On The Move: Oregon Football," Eugene Register-Guard, October 18, 2009, p. C1.

18   Chris Dufresne, "At Oregon, it's all about moving quickly and saving time," Los Angeles Times, October 20, 2010.

19   "@Chipisms" Twitter feed, October 18, 2011.

20   Don Banks, "Kelly's fast-break approach with Eagles polar opposite of Reid's," Sports Illustrated, June 5, 2013.

21   Full Chip Kelly transcript from NFL Annual Meeting.

22   Tim McManus, "Eagles Wake-Up Call: Graham Riding the New Wave," Birds 24/7, Philly Magazine online, May 30, 2013.

23   Jeffrey Martin, "If the bill fits …," USA Today, August 21, 2012.

PERSONNEL

24   Bo Wulf, "Eagles Add QB G.J. Kinne," PhiladelphiaEagles.com, March 5, 2013.

25   Chip Kelly, Signing Day press conference, February 2, 2012.

26   Mark Saltveit, "Is Michael Vick the new Darron Thomas?" Bleeding Green Nation, May 19, 2013.

27   "Mariota named Pac-12 Offensive Freshman of the

Year," Honolulu Star-Advertiser, November 26, 2012.

28   Chris Wesseling, "Ex-Eagle Nnamdi Asomugha joins San Francisco 49ers," NFL.com, March 2, 2013.

29   Spike Eskin, "Nnamdi Asomugha Used to Eat Lunch in His Car during Practice," CBS Philly website, February 26, 2013.

30   "Full Transcript: Eagles' Chip Kelly talks Peters, Barkley, Phillips, and more," Philly.com, May 28, 2013.

31   Zach Berman, "QB coach sizing up Vick, Foles, and the others," Philadelphia Inquirer, May 24, 2013.

32   Jason Brewer, "Philadelphia Eagles offense resisting labels," Bleeding Green Nation, May 25, 2013.

33   Ted Miller, "The wit and wisdom of Chip Kelly," ESPN.com, December 27, 2011.

34   Chip Kelly, "Practice Organization."

35   "Chip Kelly Press Conference, 11/13/12 (video)," Eugene Register-Guard, November 13, 2012, on YouTube.

36   Full Chip Kelly transcript from NFL Annual Meeting.

37   Chipisms Twitter account, February 16, 2012.

38   Jeffrey Martin, "If the bill fits …," USA Today, August 21, 2012.

39   Charles Fischer, "Oregon Ran Sucker Plays on USC?" FishDuck.com, May 28, 2013.

40   Chipisms Twitter account, August 16, 2011.

41   Ted Miller, "At Oregon, 'tazer' spot offers options," ESPN.com, August 19, 2009.

42   "Chip Kelly Press Conference, 11/13/12 (video)," Eugene Register-Guard, November 13, 2012, on YouTube.

43   Matt Prehm, "Chip Kelly Transcript" (from media session after first spring practice), Duck Territory website, March 28, 2011.

44   Rob Moseley, "Less disguise meant more bells and whistles against Pack," Eugene Register-Guard, September 14, 2011, p. C1.

PRACTICE

45   Mike Zhe, "Seacoast roots run deep for Oregon coach Chip Kelly," SeaCoast Online (New Hampshire), January

9, 2011.

46   Bradley Parks, "Oregon not just one-team state," NCAA.
      com, October 9, 2012.

47   Jeffrey Martin, "If the bill fits …," USA Today, August
      21, 2012.

48   Chris McPherson, "Chip Kelly: There's Much Work To
      Be Done," PhiladelphiaEagles.com, May 28, 2013.

49   Adam Jude, "Chip Kelly's Oregon offense scoring
      faster than ever, testing Ducks' limits and opponents'
      stomachs," the Oregonian, September 6, 2012.

50   Chipisms Twitter acount, October 26, 2012.

51   Chip Kelly, "Practice organization.".

52   Tim McManus, "Chip Kelly On DeSean, Science And
      the Schuylkill," Birds 24/7 blog at Philly.com, March
      20, 2013.

53   Lenn Robbins, "Kelly's winding road leads Ducks to
      top," New York Post, October 30, 2010.

54   Chipisms Twitter account, November 2, 2012.

55   Ducks' press conference after the Oregon – Oregon
      State "Civil War" game, 2009, on YouTube: "Chip Kelly
      Waters The Bamboo!" by duckswintheday1

-     Greg Bell has written a book called "Water The
      Bamboo®: Unleashing The Potential Of Teams And
      Individuals," and has a website at www.waterthebamboo.
      com.

56   ibid.

STRATEGY

57   Tim McManus, "In Chip Kelly's System, Much Is Asked
      Of the Tight Ends," Birds 24/7 blog, Philly.com, May
      25, 2013.

58   Full Chip Kelly transcript from NFL Annual Meeting.

59   "New Hampshire Coordinator Picked to Head Oregon
      Offense," GoDucks.com, February 9, 2007.

60   Chipisms Twitter account, January 8, 2011.

61   Full Chip Kelly transcript from NFL Annual Meeting.

62   Chris Brown, "The Total Package: How modern
      offenses are rethinking the most fundamental elements
      of football 'plays,'" Grantland.com, August 21, 2012.

63   Chris Brown, "Combining quick passes, run plays and

screens in the same play," SmartFootball.com, October 14, 2011.

64   Pete Thamel, "Oregon and Coach Are Over Opener," New York Times, November 1, 2009.

65   Associated Press, "No. 10 Ducks hand No. 5 Trojans worst loss since '97," ESPN.com, October 31, 2009.

66   Jeff Miller, "Trojans didn't see this one coming," Orange County Register, October 31, 2009.

67   Bruce Jenkins, "Oregon's Chip Kelly seems to coach without fear," San Francisco Chronicle, November 13, 2011.

68   Full Chip Kelly transcript from NFL Annual Meeting.

69   Full Chip Kelly transcript from NFL Annual Meeting.

70   Ibid.

71   "Chip Kelly Press Conference, 11/13/12 (video)," Eugene Register-Guard, November 13, 2012, on YouTube.

MOTIVATION

72   Chip Kelly, "Efficient use of practice time."

73   "Chip Kelly s weekly press conference (video)," posted by Rob Moseley, Eugene Register-Guard, November 22, 2011.

74   Molly Blue, "Oregon Ducks football: Chip Kelly on rivalries and SpongeBob SquarePants (videos)," the Oregonian, October 2, 2012.

75   Jason Cole, "Michael Vick Q&A, Part 2: Warned by older friend that prison was in his future," Yahoo Sports, May 14, 2013.

76   Rob Moseley, "Chip Kelly s weekly press conference (video)," Eugene Register-Guard, November 22, 2011.

77   Chipisms Twitter account, August 28, 2012.

78   "Pacific-12 Conference Championship Game: Oregon v UCLA" (press conference transcript), ASAP Sports. com, December 2, 2011.

79   Mark Saltveit, "Is Chip Kelly A Good Loser?" IgglesBlitz. com, July 18, 2013.

80   "Chip Kelly s weekly press conference (video)," posted by Rob Moseley, Eugene Register-Guard, November 22, 2011.

81   "Full Transcript: Eagles coach Chip Kelly addresses media after first day of OTAs," Philly.com, May 13, 2013.

82   Chipisms Twitter account, September 17, 2011.

83   "Seacoast roots run deep for Oregon coach Chip Kelly."

84   Vittorio Tafur, "Early troubles like water off Ducks' backs," San Francisco Chronicle, November 2, 2009.

85   Rob Moseley, "Amid opening night storylines for Oregon, biggest is debut of Marcus Mariota," Eugene Register-Guard blog, August 31, 2012.

86   Stephen Alexander, "Mariota stakes his claim to be Oregon's starting quarterback," Portland Tribune, April 28, 2012

87   ibid.

88   ibid.

89   Patrick Malee, "Local boy style: Marcus Mariota has always led by example, and that won't change as he fights for a starting job this fall," Eugene Daily Emerald, August 15, 2012.

90   Don Banks, "Kelly's fast-break approach with Eagles polar opposite of Reid's," Sports Illustrated, June 5, 2013.

91   Brian Baldinger and Harry Mayes, "Eagles Center Jason Kelce Tells Baldy And Mayes That Chip Kelly Is A Lot Easier To Communicate With Than It Was With Andy Reid," 97.5 The Fanatic Sports Radio Philadelphia, May 14, 2013.

92   Associated Press, "LSU Takes Advantage of Miscues to Best Oregon," ESPN.com, September 3, 2011.

93   Patrick Malee, "Chip Kelly's best quotes of the 2011 season," Eugene Daily Emerald, January 9, 2012.

CHIP

94   Chipisms Twitter account, July 25, 2012.

95   Austin Murphy, "Inside Rob Beard's big bunt," Sports Illustrated, October 8, 2010.

96   Tim Livingston, "How Oregon Coach Chip Kelly Can Spark 'Moneyball' Revolution In NFL," The Post Game. com, November 2, 2012.

97   Ted Miller, "The wit and wisdom of Chip Kelly," ESPN. com, December, 27, 2011.

98   Full Chip Kelly transcript from NFL Annual Meeting.

99   Tim McManus, "Chip Kelly On DeSean, Science And the Schuylkill," Birds 24/7 blog at Philly.com, March 20, 2013.

100   Full Chip Kelly transcript from NFL Annual Meeting.

101   "Full Transcript: Eagles' Chip Kelly talks Peters, Barkley, Phillips, and more," Philly.com, May 28, 2013.

102   Chipisms Twitter account, August 26, 2011.

103   Transcript of press conference before the NCG game, by Dennis Washington, at wave3.com, January 9, 2011.

104   "Pacific-12 Conference Championship Game: Oregon v UCLA" (press conference transcript), ASAP Sports. com, December 2, 2011.

105   "Chip Kelly Transcript" (from media session after first spring practice), by Matt Prehm, Duck Territory website, March 28, 2011.

106   "Seacoast roots run deep for Oregon coach Chip Kelly."

107   ibid.

108   ibid.

109   ibid.

110   Stephen Alexander, "Chip Kelly holds court, minus assistant coaches," Portland Tribune, December 31, 2011.

111   Chipisms Twitter account, January 30, 2012.

112   DuckFBNews, "Chip Kelly 2012 Recruiting Press Conference PART 1," YouTube, February 2, 2012.

113   Michael Sokolove, "Speed Freak Football," The New York Times Sunday Magazine, December 2, 2010

114   Prof. Stephen Bokenkamp, "Early Daoist Scriptures," (Berkeley: U. California Press), 1999, 2-15.

115   Tommy Lawlor, "Players, Not Positions," IgglesBlitz. com, May 3, 2013.

116   Josh Schlichter, "Fiesta Bowl No-Huddle Dynamics," FishDuck.com, January 22, 2013.

117   Charles Fischer, personal interview, May 2013.

118   Chip Kelly, "The Zone Read Option Game."

119   Gia-Fu Feng and Jane English, "Chuang Tsu Inner Chapters: A New Translation," (New York: Vintage Books), 1974, 55.

120   Chris Brown, "The New Old School," Grantland.com,

November 14, 2012.

121 Chipisms Twitter account, December 10, 2010.

122 Scott Reid, "Oregon keeps an even keel," Orange County Register, October 10, 2010.

123 Ted Miller, "Arizona State a 'huge game' for Kelly, Ducks," ESPN.com, October 18, 2012.

124 Thomas Merton, "The Way of Chuang Tzu," (Boston: Shambhala Library), 2004, 125-6.

125 Thomas Neumann, "Oregon Ducks coach Chip Kelly: Q&A," ESPN.com, August 25, 2011.

ACKNOWLEDGMENTS

I'd like to thank Brian Smith, Miriam Wolf, Noreen Kelly S.M., Dallyn Pavey, Rita Rosenkranz, Robin Michalisko, Audrey Fine Marsh, Dave Williford at the University of Oregon, Charles Fischer at FishDuck.com, Jason Brewer at Bleeding Green Nation, Jose Cazares and Forrest Johnson at Powell's Books, and Joseph Stout at World Cup Coffee for their invaluable help with this project.

ABOUT THE AUTHOR

Mark Saltveit founded and ran BCT, Inc., an innovative computer training company based in San Francisco in the 1990s. Since moving to Portland in 2001, he has worked as a consultant, writer, and stand-up comedian while raising his family.

Saltveit, a graduate of Harvard University, covers Chip Kelly and the Eagles for FishDuck.com (an Oregon Ducks strategy website) and the Philadelphia Eagles websites Bleeding Green Nation and Iggles Blitz. He has written for the *San Francisco Bay Guardian*, the *Oregonian*, *Harvard Magazine*, his own website Taoish.org, and Warp Weft and Way, an academic blog of Chinese philosophy.

He is also the World Palindrome Champion.

FOR MORE. VISIT WWW.TAOISH.ORG
AND WWW.THETAOOFCHIPKELLY.COM

CPSIA information can be obtained at www.ICGtesting.com
Printed in the USA
BVOW11s1246170614

356560BV00003B/3/P